NEW English Adventure

Student's Book with Workbook

LEVEL 1

Regina Raczyńska
Cristiana Bruni
with José Luis Morales

Pearson

Pearson Education Limited
Edinburgh Gate
Harlow
Essex CM20 2JE
England
and Associated Companies throughout the world.

www.pearsonELT.com

© Pearson Education Limited 2015. This edition of New English Adventure Level 1 is published by Pearson Education do Brasil, 2016, by arrangement of Pearson Education Limited.

Copyright © 2016 Disney Enterprises, Inc. All rights reserved. Pixar characters and artwork Copyright © Disney and Pixar.

Mr. and Mrs. Potato Head ® are registered trademarks of Hasbro, Inc. Used with permission. © Hasbro, Inc. All rights reserved.

Slinky ® Dog is a registered trademark of Poof-Slinky, Inc. © Poof-Slinky, Inc.

The rights of Regina Raczyńska and Cristiana Bruni to be identified as authors of this work have been asserted by them in accordance with the Copyright, Designs and Patents Act 1988.

Additional material provided by Jose Luis Morales.

All rights reserved; no part of this publication may be reproduced, stored in a retrieval system, or transmitted in any form or by any means, electronic, mechanical, photocopying, recording, or otherwise without the prior written permission of the Publishers.

First published 2016

ISBN 978-1-292-14107-7

Set in Frutiger Lt Pro (75 Black, 55 Roman)

Printed in Brazil

Head of Product- Pearson Brazil: Gabriela Diuana
Product Manager- Pearson Brazil: Marjorie Robles
Product Coordinator: Priscila Marconi
Design Coordinator: Cleber Carvalho
MediaHub- Pearson Brazil
Author: Regina Racznska, Cristiana Bruni with José Luis Morales
Editors: Rhiannon Ball and Priscila Marconi
Art and Design: Alto Contraste SP
Audio: Maximal Studio
Media Development: Estação Gráfica

Pearson Education Brazil would like to thank Gisele Aga for her contribution during the development of the series.

Illustrated by Fran and David Brylewski, Sean Parkes.
Cartoons: pg 8 duckworks, F. Guell, A. Rodriguez (Comicup), F. Rodriguez, Y. TebarComic; pg 16 duckworks, U. Schröder, A. Rodriguez (Comicup), F. Rodriguez, Y. TebarComic; pg 24 duckworks, U. Schröder, A. Rodriguez (Comicup), F. Rodriguez, Y. TebarComic; pg 32 duckworks, F. Guell, A. Rodriguez (Comicup), F. Rodriguez, Y. TebarComic; pg 40 duckworks, D. Jippes, F. Rodriguez, Y.TebarComic; pg 48 duckworks, F. Guell, A. Rodriguez (Comicup), F. Rodriguez, Y. TebarComic; pg 56 duckworks, U. Schröder, A. Rodriguez (Comicup), F. Rodriguez, Y. TebarComic; pg 64 duckworks, D. Jippes, F. Guell, F. Rodriguez, Y. Tebar.

The publisher would like to thank the following for their kind permission to reproduce their photographs:

(Key: b-bottom; c-centre; l-left; r-right; t-top)

Alamy Images: Hermesmereghettistud 34bl, Kitch Bain 50tl, Koch Valérie 26bl; **DK Images:** Peter Anderson 68c; **Pawel Ferenc:** 21tr; **Fotolia.com:** 3drenderings 26tc, a7880ss 37tr, Africa Studio 58 (cakes), 70cr, AK-DigiArt 71l, aleksandrn 34br, Alis Photo 50 (car), Aaron Amat 50 (controller), Anatolii 70l, Anyka 70r, atoss 53 (pears), 53tl, 53tr, 58 (bananas), 58 (orange), 58 (pears), babimu 3cl, Beboy 52l, 85bl, Matthew Benoit 3l, bluebat 44r, 83 (teddy), bluefern 50bl, brites_99 21br, Coprid 34bc, design56 21l, DeVIce 60c, 66tl, Dinga 3c, Dionisvera 58 (carrots), DLVV 72r, Neo Edmund 26br, eldadcarin 18bl, elovich 58 (tomatoes), examphotos 26tl, gekaskr 18tr, Gelpi 3cr, Ivan Gusev 45/2, 83 (kite), Shawn Hempel 54r, 85cl, homydesign 69cl, ibphoto 50 (plastic blocks), Ichbins11 26tr, Irochka 29/5, Eric Isselée 36cr, itsmejust 60l, Valeriy Ivashchenko 44cl, 83tr, jdwfoto 66b, jojje11 69l, joppo 45/3, 83 (yo-yo), karandaev 29/2, Alexia Khruscheva 29/1, kittipak 37tc, 37bl, 37br, Kitty 68r, Kletr 36r, koleg68 50tr, Volodymyr Krasyuk 52cl, 85cr, kreatorex 50 (robot), Anna Kucherova 58tl, M.studio 58 (juice), mariesacha 44l, 83tl, Sergio Martínez 58 (chicken), 58 (eggs), Mexrix 34cr, michaklootwijk 3r, Alexandr Mitiuc 69r, mrjpeg 54c, 85 (eggs), Natika 58 (cheese), 58tc, Stefano Neri 50 (jigsaw), ninell 69cr, nui7711 45/1, 83 (car), Leonid Nyshko 34cl, oriori 52cr, 58 (milk), 85 (milk), paffy 71c, Perseomedusa 60r, Uros Petrovic 71r, PhotographyByMK 18c, Brad Pict 66tr, piopis 85 (oranges), robert 29/3, robert6666 52r, 85tl, Schlierner 21tc, Michael Shake 18cr, simmittorok 50 (marbles), simonkr 50 (plastic chest), Smileus 34c, 68l, 69c, sombra_de_luna 36l, srdjan111 18bc, stavrida 50 (wooden blocks), Stock Creative 50 (horse), Dmytro Sukharevskyy 50 (helicopter), Szasz-Fabian Erika 1ºbr, t2sk5 45/4, 83bl, Denis Tabler 29/4, Tatik22 70cl, tempakul 44cr, 83br, Tiler84 54l, 58 (bread), 85tr, Torbz 71cl, 71cr, Nikolai Tsvetkov 50 (train), valery121283 53 (apples), 58 (apples), 58tr, 85 (pears), 85br, Vasily 50br, _Vilor 72l, Ivonne Wierink 50 (wooden train), Robert Wilson 18cl, yellowj 37tl; **Getty Images:** sarahwolfephotography 18tl; **Imagemore Co., Ltd:** 36cl; **Pearson Education Ltd:** Rafal Trubisz 5l, 5cl, 5cr, 5r, 9, 10tl, 10tc, 10tr, 10c, 10cl, 10cr, 10bl, 10bc, 10br, 17l, 17r, 25, 33, 34tl, 34tc, 34tr, 41, 45tl, 49tl, 49tr, 49c, 49bl, 49br, 53b, 57tl, 57tc, 57tr, 57c, 57cl, 57cr, 57bl, 57br, 65; **SuperStock:** Design Pics 72cl, 72cr

All other images © Pearson Education

Every effort has been made to trace the copyright holders and we apologise in advance for any unintentional omissions. We would be pleased to insert the appropriate acknowledgement in any subsequent edition of this publication.

NEW English Adventure

LEVEL 1

CONTENTS	PAGE
HELLO	2
1. MY BODY	4
2. MY FAMILY	12
3. MY CLASSROOM	20
4. ANIMALS	28
5. THE SEA	36
6. TOYS	44
7. FOOD	52
8. MY VACATION	60

CONTENTS	PAGE
HAPPY EASTER!	68
MERRY CHRISTMAS!	70
FAMILY DAY	72
CUT-OUTS	73
STICKERS	89
POSTER ACTIVITY	93
WORKBOOK	97
PICTURE DICTIONARY	167
STICKERS	169

HELLO

1 LISTEN AND CHANT. CD 1.6 🎵 KARAOKE CD 1.7

2 LISTEN AND STICK. CD 1.8 sticker

3 FIND AND CHECK (✓). ✏️

HELLO: BLUE, GREEN, RED, YELLOW

4 LISTEN AND CIRCLE.

5 FIND AND COLOR.

HELLO: PINK, *BLUE, GREEN, RED, YELLOW*

UNIT 1 MY BODY

1 LISTEN AND CHANT. CD 1.10 🎵 KARAOKE CD 1.11

2 LISTEN AND STICK. CD 1.12

3 FIND AND CHECK (✓).

VOCABULARY I: BODY, FEET, HANDS, HEAD. MY (BODY)

4

4 LISTEN AND SAY. THEN LISTEN AND CIRCLE.

5 MATCH. THEN SAY.

VOCABULARY II: CLAP YOUR HANDS, MOVE YOUR BODY, STAMP YOUR FEET, TOUCH YOUR HEAD. *BODY.*

6 LISTEN AND CHANT. THEN MATCH. CD 1.14 ♪ CD 1.15 KARAOKE

1 2 3 4 5

7 LISTEN AND SING. CD 1.16 ♪ CD 1.17 KARAOKE

SONG: 1-5. (TWO) (FEET). BODY. COLORS. IMPERATIVES.

UNIT 1

④ ⑤

⑧ LOOK AND SAY. THEN COUNT AND DRAW.

7

9 LISTEN AND ANSWER. 🎵 CD 1.18 💬

10 NOW ACT THE STORY OUT. 💬

STORY: *BODY. COLORS. NUMBERS.*

11 LISTEN AND DRAW. THEN SAY. CD 1.19

12 GO TO PAGE 73. CUT OUT. THEN LISTEN AND PLAY. CD 1.20

SKILLS: *BODY. IMPERATIVES. NUMBERS.*

UNIT 1

13 LISTEN AND CIRCLE WITH ◯ OR ◯. THEN MATCH.

14 LOOK AND SAY. THEN COLOR.

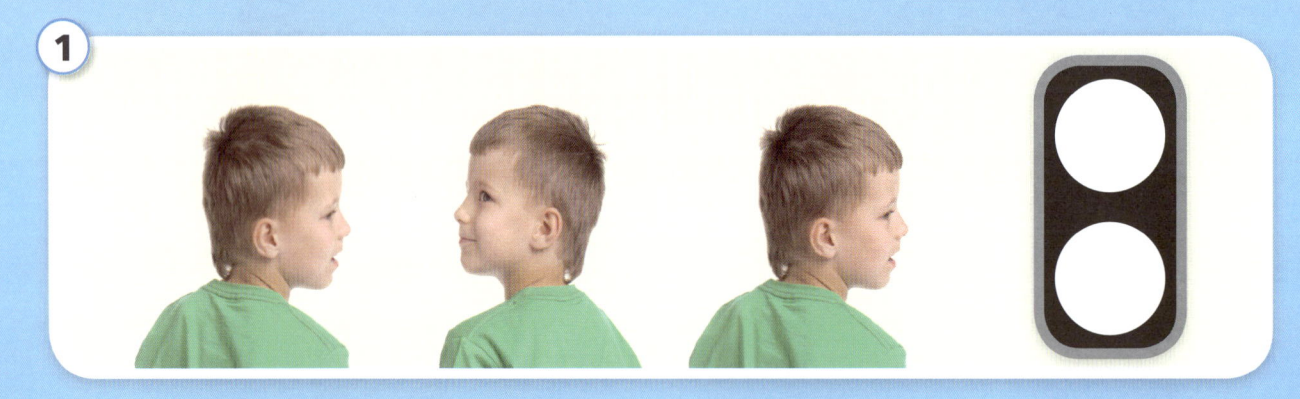

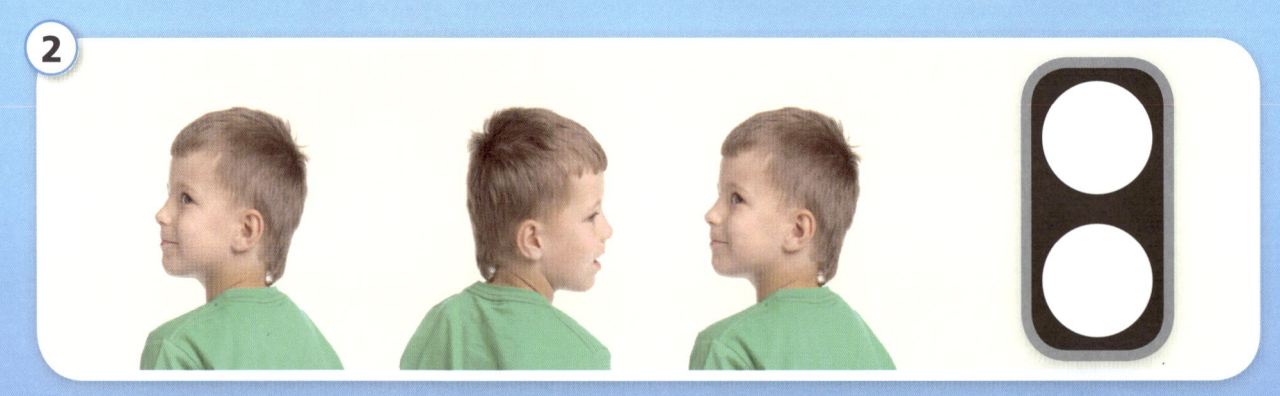

15 MAKE A POSTER.

CLIL: LEFT, RIGHT. MY (LEFT) (HAND).

REVIEW 1

1 **LISTEN AND CHECK (✓).** CD 1.22

REVIEW 1: BODY. COLORS. IMPERATIVES. NUMBERS.

UNIT 2 MY FAMILY

1 LISTEN AND CHANT.

2 LISTEN AND STICK.

3 FIND AND CHECK (✓).

VOCABULARY I: BROTHER, DAD, MOM, SISTER. THIS IS MY (FAMILY).

4 LISTEN AND CIRCLE. CD 1.26

5 LOOK AT ACTIVITY 4 AND COLOR. THEN PLAY.

VOCABULARY II: FRIEND, GRANDMA, GRANDPA. COLORS. FAMILY. THIS IS MY (BROTHER).

13

6 LISTEN AND POINT. THEN SAY. CD 1.27

7 LISTEN AND SING. CD 1.28 CD 1.29 KARAOKE

SONG: JUMP, RUN, TURN AROUND. *FAMILY. THIS IS MY (MOM).*

14

UNIT 2

8 FIND AND CHECK (✓). THEN SAY.

15

9 LISTEN AND ANSWER. CD 1.30

10 NOW ACT THE STORY OUT.

STORY: *IMPERATIVES. THIS IS ...*

16

UNIT 2

11 MATCH. THEN SAY.

12 GO TO PAGE 75. CUT OUT. THEN LISTEN AND PLAY.

SKILLS: *FAMILY. IMPERATIVES.*

17

13 LISTEN AND CHECK (✓). THEN SAY.

CD 1.32

1

2

14 MATCH AND CIRCLE WITH ◯ OR ◯.

1

2

3

4

5

6

15 MAKE A POSTER.

CLIL: BIG, SMALL. FAMILY. THIS IS MY (SISTER).

18

REVIEW 2

1 LISTEN AND CHECK (✓) OR CROSS (✗). THEN SAY. CD 1.33

2 DRAW AND SAY.

REVIEW 2: *FAMILY.*

UNIT 3
MY CLASSROOM

1 LISTEN AND CHANT. CD 1.34 ♪ KARAOKE CD 1.35

2 LISTEN AND STICK. CD 1.36 stick

3 FIND AND CHECK (✓).

VOCABULARY I: CHAIR, PEN, PENCIL, TABLE. PICK UP A (PEN). POINT TO A (CHAIR).

20

4 LISTEN, POINT AND SAY.
THEN LISTEN AND CHECK (✓) OR CROSS (✗). CD 1.37

5 LOOK AND COLOR. THEN SAY.

VOCABULARY II: BAG, BOOK, CRAYON, ERASER. A (RED) (BOOK). *COLORS. NUMBERS. SCHOOL OBJECTS.*

6 LISTEN AND COLOR. CD 1.38

1

2

SONG: A (BIG) (BAG). *BIG, SMALL. COLORS. SCHOOL OBJECTS. A (RED) (BOOK).*

22

UNIT 3

7 **LISTEN AND SING.** CD 1.39 CD 1.40 KARAOKE

8 **LISTEN AND CIRCLE. THEN SAY.** CD 1.41

23

9 LISTEN AND ANSWER. CD 1.42

10 NOW ACT THE STORY OUT.

STORY: YOUR (BAG), PLEASE. HERE YOU ARE. *BIG, SMALL. COLORS. SCHOOL OBJECTS. A (SMALL) (BAG). A (RED) (BOOK).*

11 LISTEN, COLOR AND DRAW. THEN SAY. 🎧 1.43

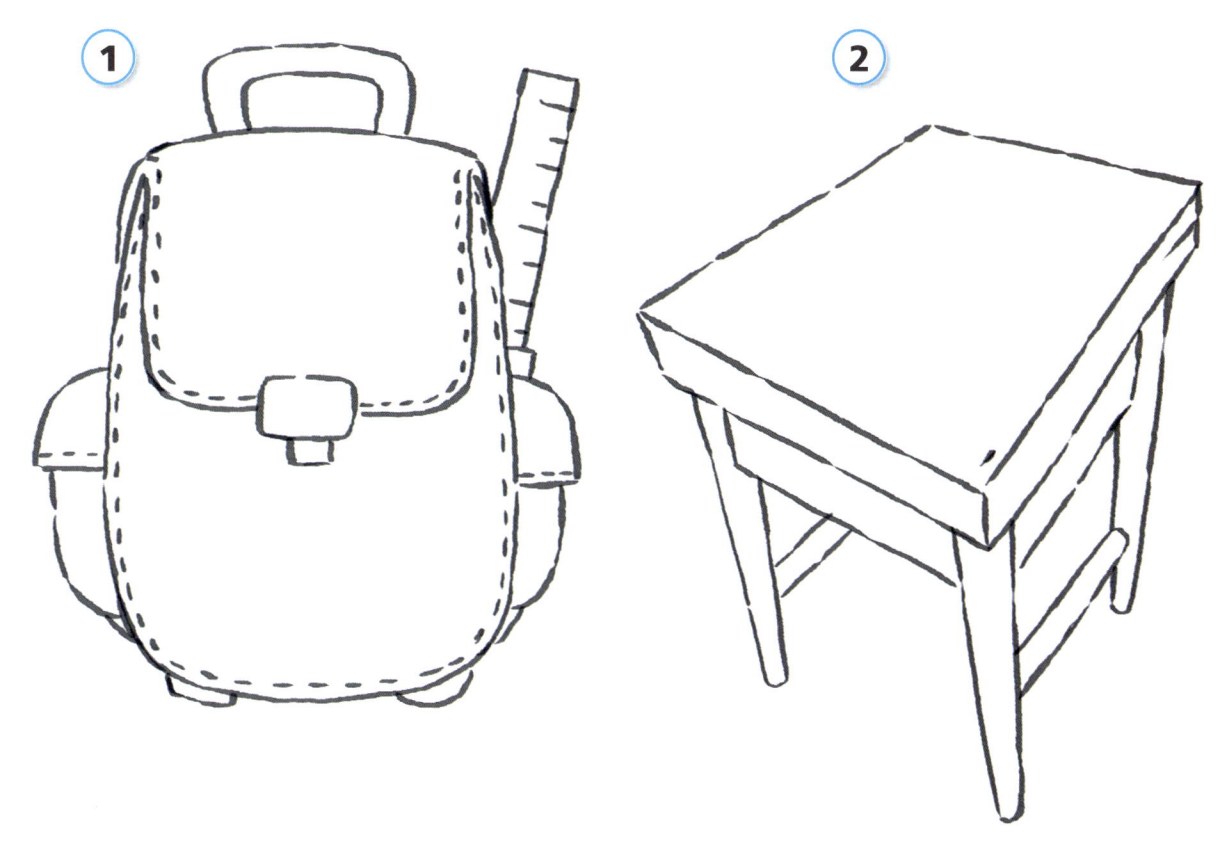

1

2

12 GO TO PAGE 77. CUT OUT. THEN LISTEN AND PLAY. ✂️ 🎧 1.44

UNIT **3**

SKILLS: *BIG, SMALL. COLORS. SCHOOL OBJECTS. A (SMALL) (BAG). A (RED) (BOOK).*

25

13 LISTEN, POINT AND SAY. THEN CHECK (✔) OR CROSS (✘). CD 1.45

1 2 3 4

14 LISTEN AND CIRCLE. THEN SAY. CD 1.46

1

2

15 MAKE A POSTER.

CLIL: BOARD, CARPET, DESK. *BIG, SMALL.* SCHOOL OBJECTS. A (SMALL) (CHAIR).

26

REVIEW 3

1 LISTEN AND CHECK (✓). THEN SAY. CD 1.47

2 DRAW AND SAY.

REVIEW 3: *BIG, SMALL. COLORS. SCHOOL OBJECTS. A (SMALL) (BAG). A (RED) (BOOK).*

UNIT 4 ANIMALS

1 LISTEN AND CHANT. CD 1.48 CD 1.49 KARAOKE

2 LISTEN AND STICK. CD 1.50 stick

3 COUNT AND CHECK (✓).

VOCABULARY I: 6–10. DOG. 1–5.

28

4 LISTEN AND POINT. THEN MATCH. CD 1.51

5 LOOK AND CHECK (✓) OR CROSS (✗).

1   2   3   4

VOCABULARY II: BIRD, CAT, HORSE, RABBIT, *DOG*. IT'S A (CAT).

29

6 LISTEN AND CIRCLE. CD 1.52

SONG: BLACK, WHITE, PUPPIES. BIG, SMALL. ANIMALS. NUMBERS. IT'S A (CAT).

7 LISTEN AND SING. CD 1.53 CD 1.54

8 FIND AND DRAW.

9 LISTEN AND ANSWER.

10 NOW ACT THE STORY OUT.

STORY: *BIG, SMALL. ANIMALS. COLORS. NUMBERS. IT'S A (CAT).*

UNIT 4

11 LISTEN, FIND AND CHECK (✓). THEN SAY. CD 1.56

12 GO TO PAGE 79. CUT OUT. THEN LISTEN AND PLAY. CD 1.57

SKILLS: *BIG, SMALL. ANIMALS. COLORS. NUMBERS. IT'S A (CAT).*

13 LISTEN AND MATCH. THEN SAY. CD 1.58

14 LOOK AND DRAW. THEN SAY.

15 MAKE A POSTER.

CLIL: FISH, HAMSTER, TORTOISE. *IT'S A (FISH).*

34

1 COUNT AND CIRCLE. THEN SAY.

5 / 6

2 / 1

1 / 7

4 / 9

2 DRAW AND SAY.

REVIEW 4: *BIG, SMALL. ANIMALS. COLORS. NUMBERS. IT'S A (CAT).*

REVIEW 4

UNIT 5
THE SEA

1 LISTEN AND CHANT.

2 LISTEN AND STICK.

3 FIND AND CHECK (✓).

VOCABULARY I: FISH, OCTOPUS, SEAHORSE, STARFISH. *IT'S A (FISH)*.

4 LISTEN AND CHECK. THEN SAY.

5 FOLLOW AND COLOR.

VOCABULARY II: CRAB, SHELL; BROWN, GRAY, ORANGE, PURPLE. IT'S (PURPLE). *SEA ANIMALS. IT'S A (FISH).*

37

6 LISTEN AND DRAW. CD 2.5

1
2
3
4
5

7 LISTEN AND SING. CD 2.6 KARAOKE CD 2.7

SONG: TURTLE; HAPPY, SAD. I'M (HAPPY). WE ARE HAPPY IN THE SEA. SEA ANIMALS. NUMBERS.

UNIT 5

8 COUNT AND CIRCLE.

1 2 3 4 5 6

9 LISTEN AND ANSWER. CD 2.8

10 NOW ACT THE STORY OUT.

STORY: BIG, SMALL. COLORS. SEA ANIMALS. IT'S A (CRAB). IT'S (SMALL). IT'S (GRAY).

40

UNIT 5

11 LISTEN AND DRAW. THEN SAY. CD 2.9

12 GO TO PAGE 81. CUT OUT. THEN LISTEN AND PLAY. CD 2.10

SKILLS: COLORS. NUMBERS. SEA ANIMALS. IT'S A (CRAB). IT'S (GRAY).

41

13 **LISTEN AND DRAW. THEN CIRCLE.** CD 2.11

1

2

14 **LOOK AND SAY. THEN CROSS OUT.**

15 **MAKE A POSTER.**

CLIL: BEACH, CLEAN, DIRTY. *IT'S* (CLEAN). *I'M* (HAPPY).

42

REVIEW 5

1 LISTEN AND CHECK (✓) OR CROSS (✗). THEN SAY. CD 2.12

2 DRAW AND SAY.

REVIEW 5: *HAPPY, SAD. COLORS. SEA ANIMALS. IT'S A (CRAB). IT'S (GRAY).*

43

UNIT 6 TOYS

1 LISTEN AND CHANT.

2 LISTEN AND STICK.

3 FIND AND CHECK (✓).

VOCABULARY I: BALL, BOAT, DOLL, TEDDY BEAR. *IT'S A (PURPLE)* (BALL).

44

4 LISTEN AND POINT. THEN LISTEN AND CIRCLE.

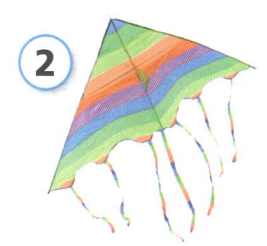

5 MATCH AND COLOR. THEN SAY.

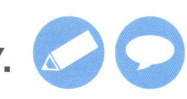

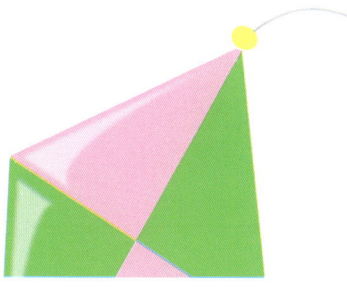

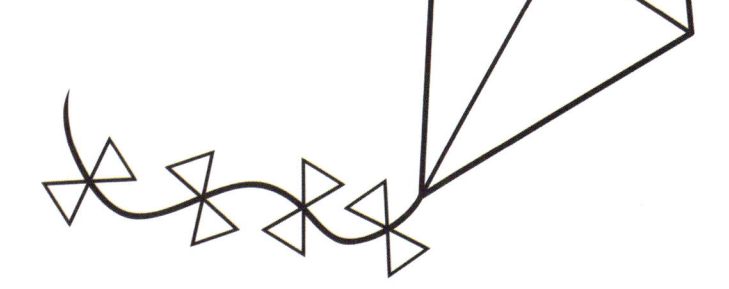

VOCABULARY II: CAR, KITE, TRAIN, YO-YO. I HAVE A (CAR). *IT'S A (KITE). IT'S (RED).*

45

6 LISTEN AND CHECK (✓) OR CROSS (✗). CD 2.17

1.
2.
3.
4.

7 LISTEN AND SING. CD 2.18 CD 2.19 KARAOKE

SONG: I HAVE A (RED) (CAR). LET'S FLY. *BIG, SMALL. TOYS. I HAVE A (CAR).*

UNIT 6

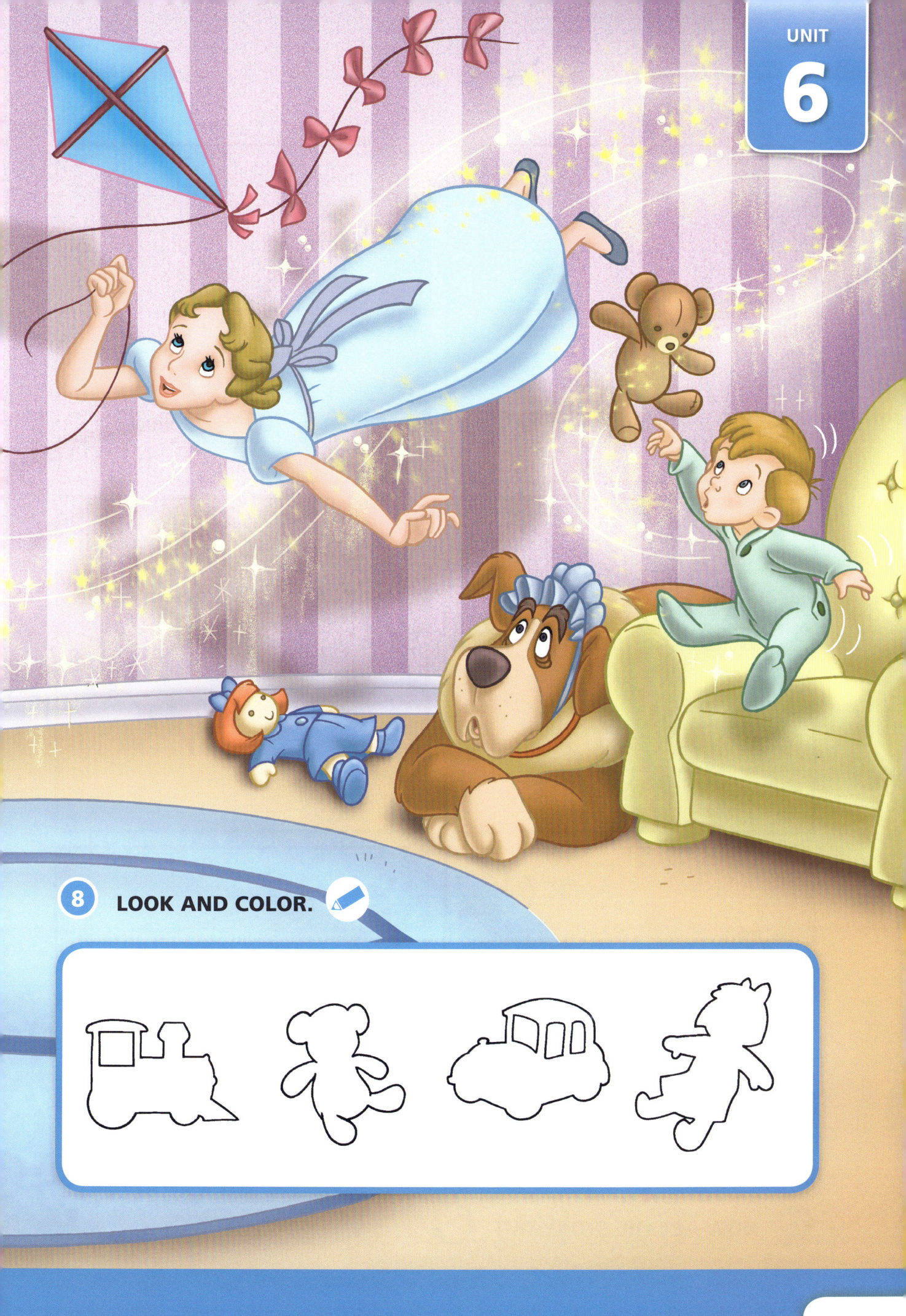

8 LOOK AND COLOR.

47

9 LISTEN AND ANSWER. CD 2.20

10 NOW ACT THE STORY OUT.

STORY: BIG, SMALL. TOYS. I HAVE A (DOLL). IT'S PINK. I HAVE A (GREEN) (CAR).

UNIT 6

11 COUNT AND MATCH.
THEN LISTEN AND CHECK (✓) OR CROSS (✗). CD 2.21

1 2 3 4 5 6

1

2

3

12 GO TO PAGE 83. CUT OUT. THEN LISTEN AND PLAY. CD 2.22

SKILLS: NUMBERS. TOYS. I HAVE A (DOLL).

49

13 LISTEN AND POINT. THEN CIRCLE WITH ◯ OR ◯.

1 2 3 4

14 MATCH. THEN SAY.

15 MAKE A POSTER.

CLIL: NEW, OLD. *I HAVE A (DOLL).*

50

REVIEW 6

1 COUNT AND CHECK (✓) OR CROSS (✗). THEN SAY.

- princess: 3 ☐
- train: 2 ☐
- car: 2 ☐
- yo-yo: 4 ☐

- ship: 5 ☐
- ball: 1 ☐
- teddy bear: 2 ☐
- kite: 5 ☐

2 DRAW AND SAY.

REVIEW 6: NUMBERS. TOYS. I HAVE A (GREEN) (CAR).

UNIT 7 FOOD

1 LISTEN AND CHANT. CD 2.24 ♪ KARAOKE CD 2.25

2 LISTEN AND STICK. CD 2.26 stick

3 FIND AND CHECK (✓).

VOCABULARY 1: CAKES, CHEESE, CHICKEN, MILK. I LIKE (CHICKEN).

52

4 LISTEN, READ AND POINT. THEN DRAW 🙂. CD 2.27

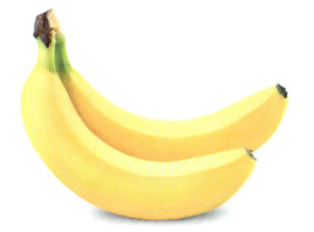

BANANAS    APPLES    PEARS    ORANGES

5 MATCH, COLOR AND SAY.

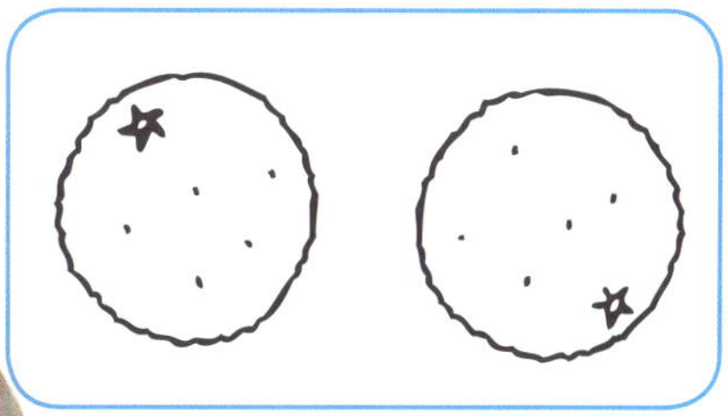

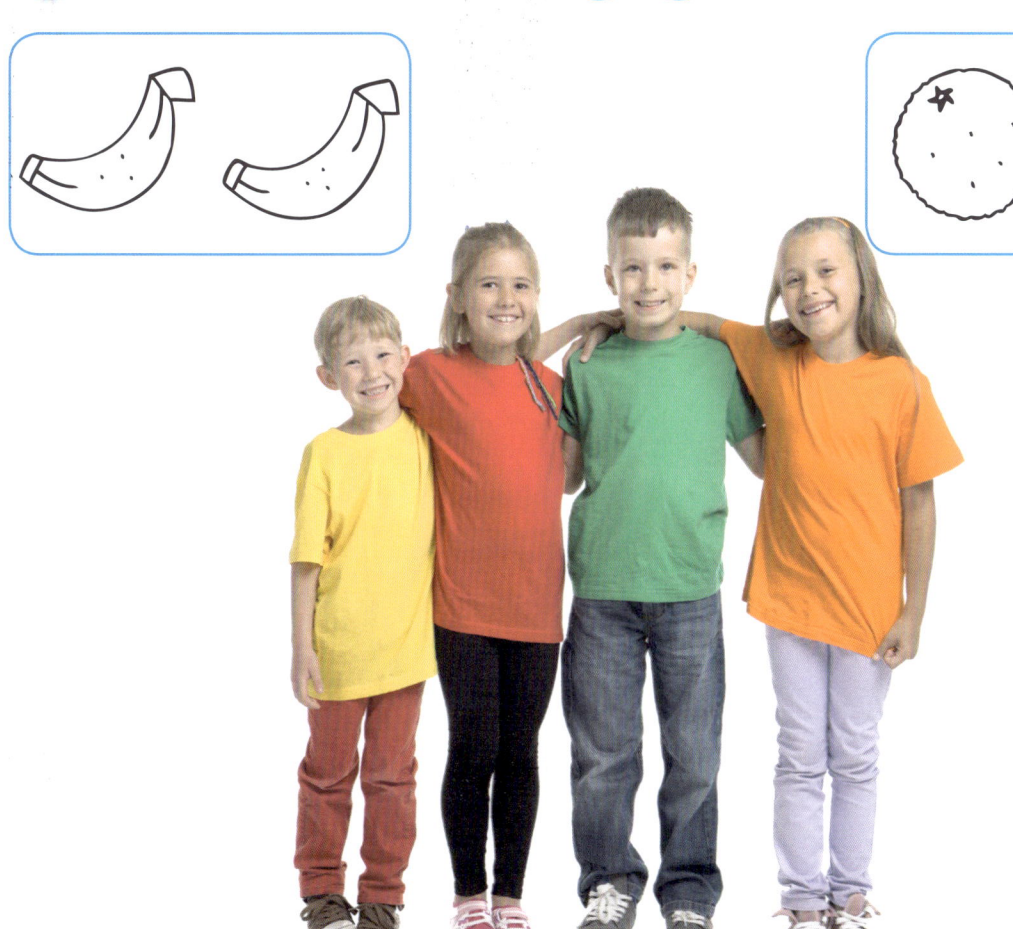

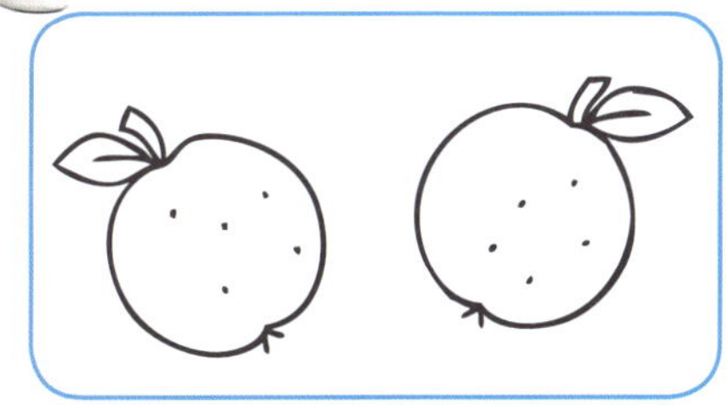

VOCABULARY II: APPLES, BANANAS, ORANGES, PEARS. *I LIKE* (APPLES).

53

6 LISTEN AND POINT. THEN LISTEN AND DRAW 🙂 OR ☹. CD 2.28

BREAD   EGGS   JUICE

SONG: BREAD, EGGS, JUICE; YUCK, YUM. I DON'T LIKE (EGGS). *FOOD. I LIKE (CHEESE).*

7 LISTEN AND SING. CD 2.29 🎵 KARAOKE CD 2.30

UNIT **7**

8 FIND AND CIRCLE. ✏️

9 **LISTEN AND ANSWER.** CD 2.31

10 **NOW ACT THE STORY OUT.**

STORY: *FOOD. I LIKE (CHEESE).*

UNIT 7

11 **LISTEN AND CIRCLE.** CD 2.32

1
2
3

12 **GO TO PAGE 85. CUT OUT. THEN LISTEN AND PLAY.** CD 2.33

SKILLS: *YUCK, YUM. FOOD. I LIKE / DON'T LIKE (CHEESE).*

57

13 LISTEN AND CHECK (✓). CD 2.34

1.

2.

14 CIRCLE WITH ◯ OR ◯. THEN SAY.

15 MAKE A POSTER.

CLIL: CARROTS, TOMATOES, GOOD FOR ME. *FOOD. I LIKE / DON'T LIKE (CHEESE).*

REVIEW 7

1 COLOR. THEN SAY.

2 LOOK, READ AND CHECK (✓) OR CROSS (✗).

1. I LIKE EGGS.
2. I DON'T LIKE MILK.
3. I DON'T LIKE APPLES.
4. I LIKE PEARS.
5. I DON'T LIKE BREAD.

REVIEW 7: YUCK, YUM. FOOD. I LIKE / DON'T LIKE (CHEESE).

UNIT 8 MY VACATION

1 LISTEN AND CHANT.

2 LISTEN AND STICK.

3 FIND AND CHECK (✓).

VOCABULARY I: BEACH, SANDCASTLE, SEA. *COLORS. NUMBERS. SEA ANIMALS.*

60

4 LISTEN AND CIRCLE. CD 2.38

5 MATCH AND SAY. THEN FIND AND DRAW.

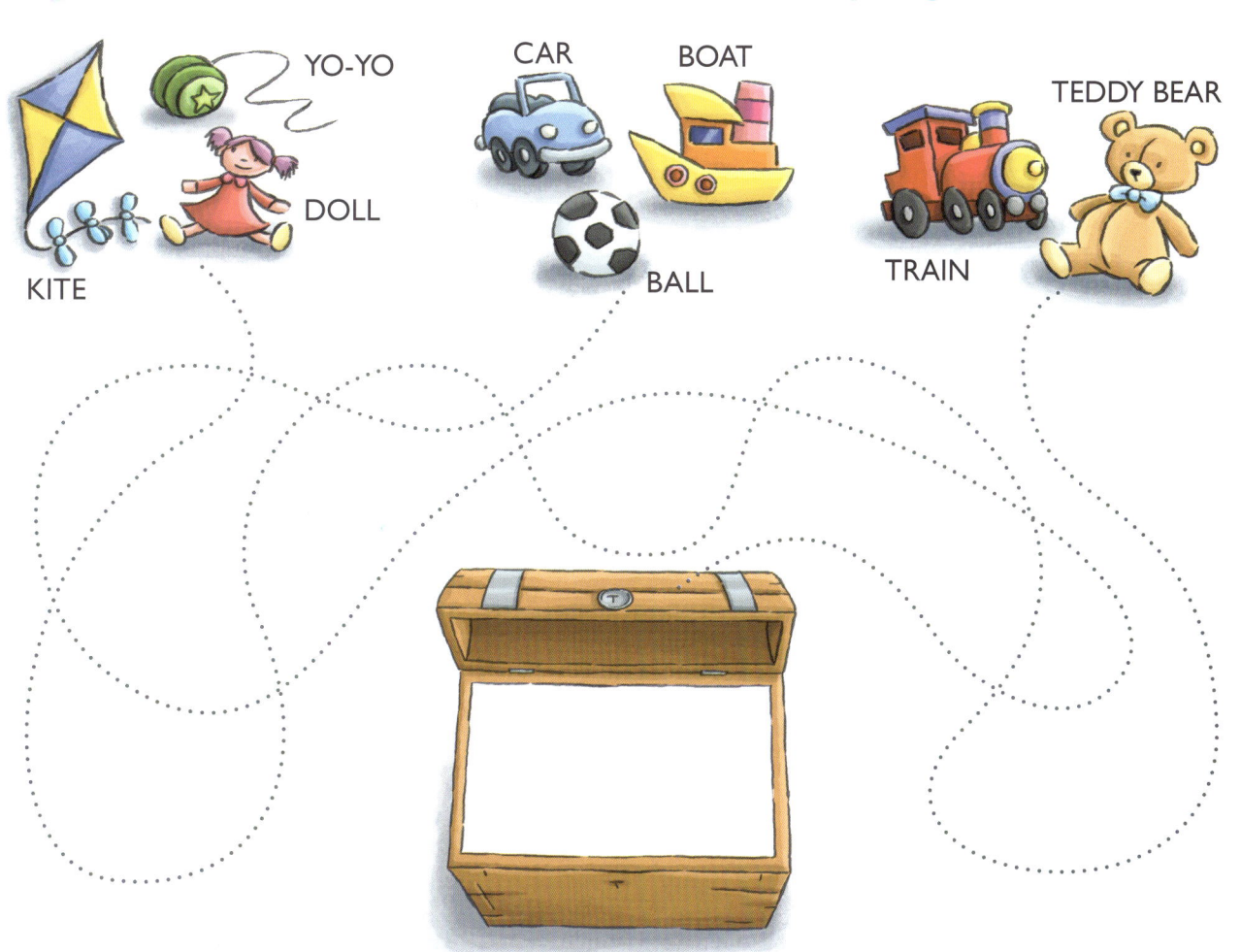

KITE YO-YO DOLL CAR BOAT BALL TRAIN TEDDY BEAR

VOCABULARY II: *COLORS. TOYS. I HAVE A (BALL). IT'S A (CAR). IT'S (BLUE). IT'S (SMALL).*

6 FIND AND CIRCLE.

7 LISTEN AND SING.

SONG: PICNIC, DELICIOUS. FOOD. NUMBERS. SEA ANIMALS. SCHOOL OBJECTS. TOYS. I LIKE / DON'T LIKE (CHEESE).

UNIT 8

8 COUNT AND DRAW.

63

9 LISTEN AND ANSWER. CD 2.41

10 NOW ACT THE STORY OUT.

STORY: *COLORS. SCHOOL OBJECTS. TOYS. IMPERATIVES.*
IT'S A (RED) (BALL). I HAVE A (BIG) (BOOK).

UNIT 8

11 **LISTEN AND CROSS OUT.** CD 2.42

1

2

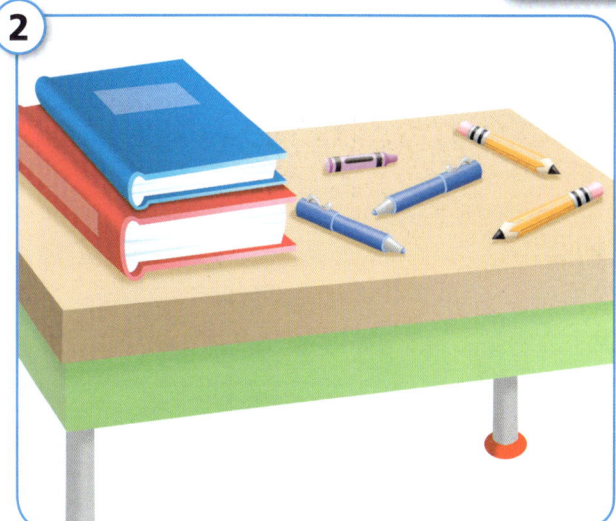

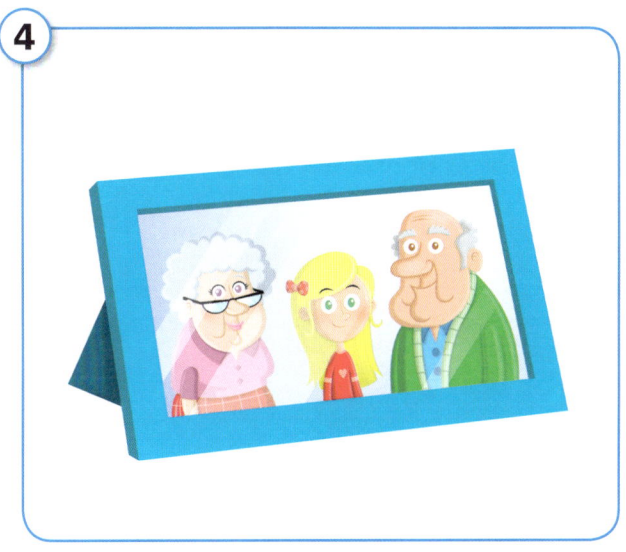

3

4

12 **GO TO PAGE 87. CUT OUT. THEN LISTEN AND PLAY.** CD 2.43

SKILLS: ANIMALS. COLORS. FAMILY. FOOD. SCHOOL OBJECTS.
I HAVE A (PEN). I LIKE (MILK).

65

13 LISTEN AND NUMBER. CD 2.44

14 LISTEN AND MATCH. CD 2.45

1
2
3

15 MAKE A POSTER.

CLIL: LAKE, MOUNTAINS, *SEA. FAMILY.*

REVIEW 8

1 COUNT AND CIRCLE. THEN READ AND SAY.

9 / 10
SHELLS

2 / 6
BALLS

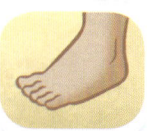

1 / 3
BIRDS

5 / 8
BANANAS

4 / 5
FEET

2 DRAW AND SAY.

REVIEW 8: ANIMALS. BODY. COLORS. FOOD. NUMBERS. SEA ANIMALS. TOYS.

67

HAPPY EASTER!

1 LISTEN, POINT AND SAY. CD 2.46

2 LISTEN AND CHECK (✓). THEN LISTEN AND SING. CD 2.47 · KARAOKE CD 2.48

SONG: BASKET, CHICK, EASTER EGG, EASTER BUNNY. *IT'S A (CHICK).*

3 LISTEN AND CHECK (✔) OR CROSS (✘).

1. CHICK ☐
2. EASTER EGG ☐
3. BASKET ☐
4. EASTER BUNNY ☐

4 COUNT AND WRITE. THEN SAY.

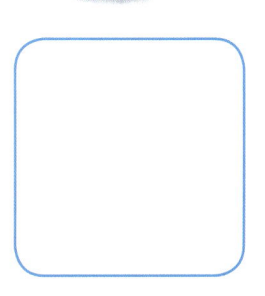

5 MAKE A POSTER.

PROJECT: *BASKET, CHICK, EASTER EGG, EASTER BUNNY. IT'S A (CHICK).*

MERRY CHRISTMAS!

1 LISTEN, POINT AND SAY. CD 2.50

2 LISTEN AND CHECK (✓). THEN LISTEN AND SING. CD 2.51 CD 2.52

SONG: CHRISTMAS CARD, CHRISTMAS TREE, SANTA CLAUS

3 LISTEN, READ AND CHECK (✓).

PRESENT ☐

STOCKING ☐

CHRISTMAS TREE ☐

BELL ☐

STAR ☐

4 CHOOSE AND COLOR.

5 MAKE A POSTER.

PROJECT: BELL, PRESENT, STAR, STOCKING. IT'S A (STAR).
CHRISTMAS CARD, CHRISTMAS TREE, SANTA CLAUS.

FAMILY DAY

1 LISTEN, READ AND CIRCLE.

1. 
FLOWER  CARD

2. 
CARD  PRESENT

2 LISTEN AND CHECK (✓). THEN LISTEN AND SING.

3 MAKE A POSTER.

SONG / PROJECT: FLOWER(S), *CARD*, *PRESENT*. FOR MY (MOM), FOR YOU. *FAMILY*.

72

Notes

Notes

Notes

Notes

Notes

Notes

UNIT 1

12 CUT OUT. THEN LISTEN AND PLAY.

1 2 3 4 5

UNIT 2

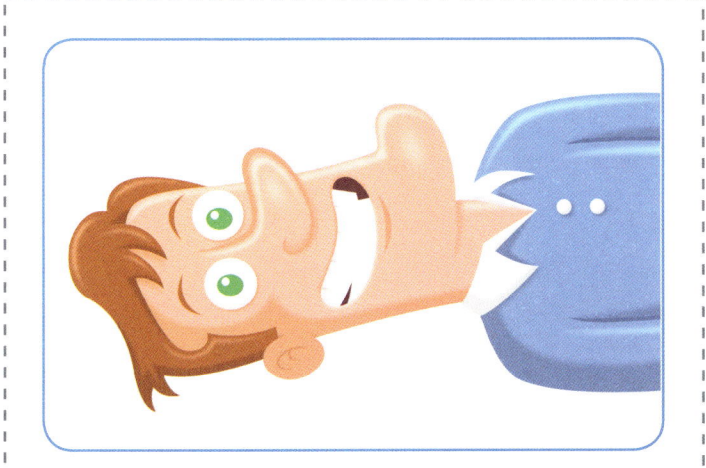

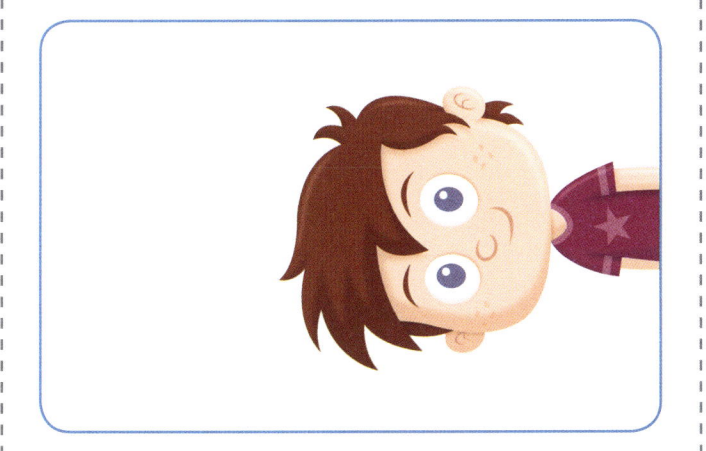

12 CUT OUT. THEN LISTEN AND PLAY.

UNIT 3

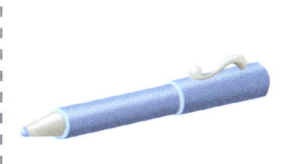

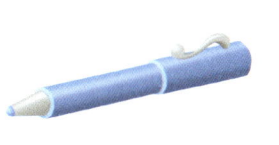

12 CUT OUT. THEN LISTEN AND PLAY.

77

UNIT 4

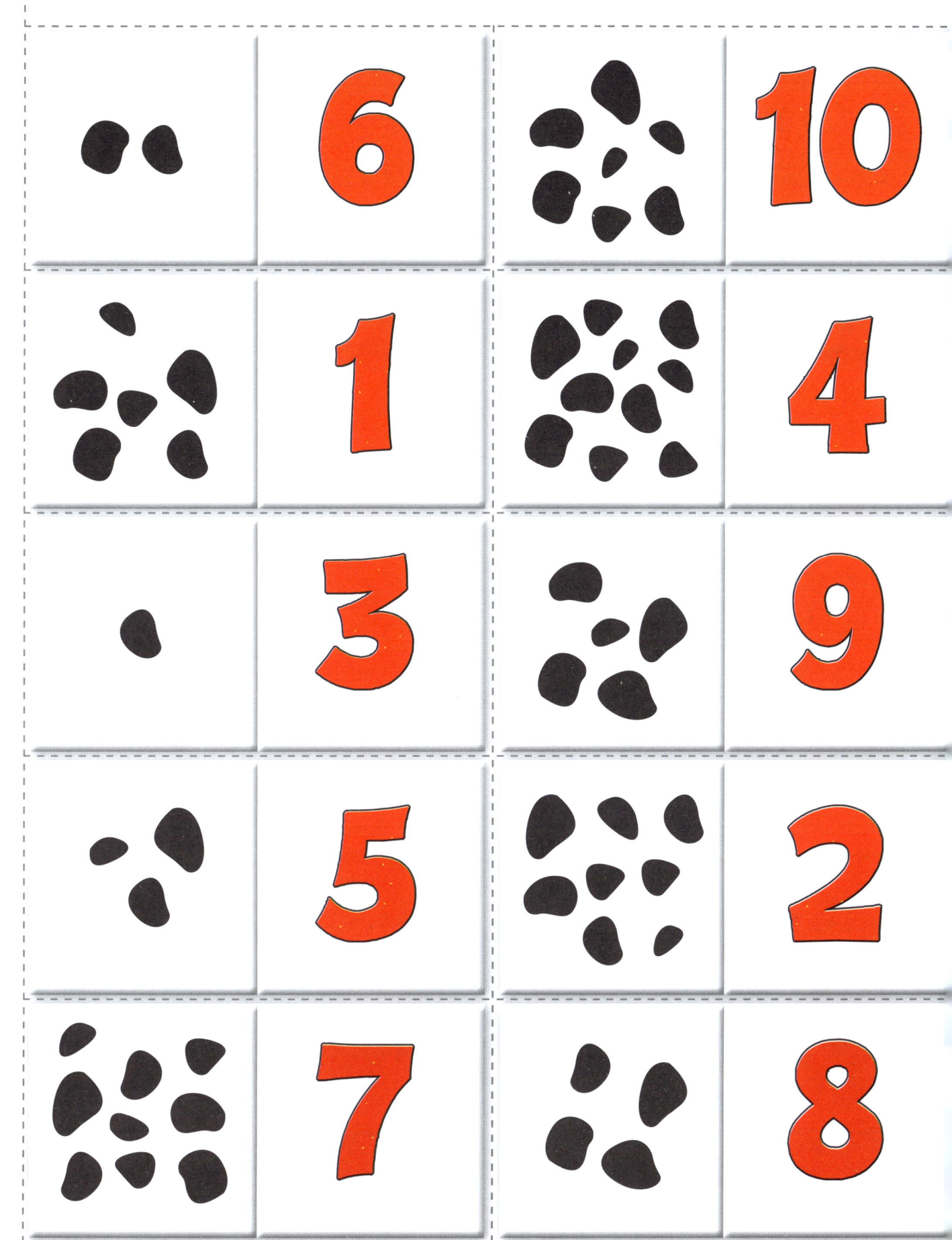

12 CUT OUT. THEN LISTEN AND PLAY.

UNIT 5

12 CUT OUT. THEN LISTEN AND PLAY.

UNIT 6

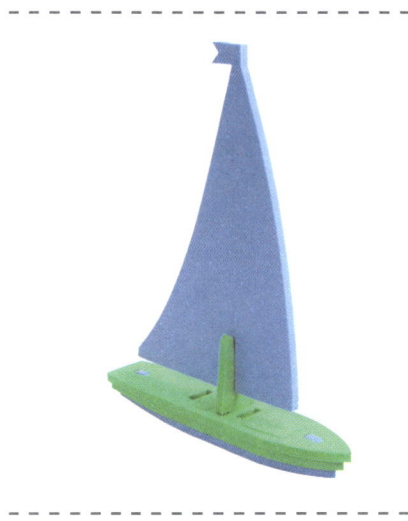

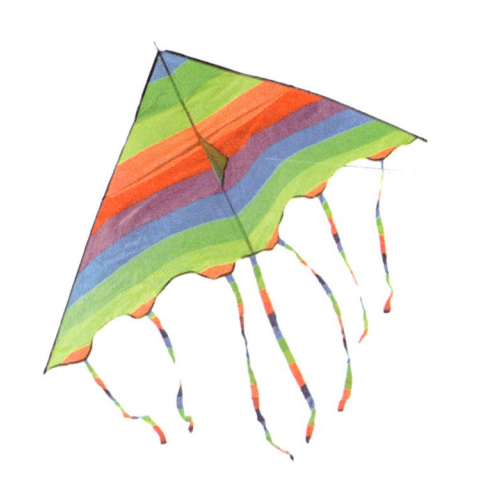

12 CUT OUT. THEN LISTEN AND PLAY.

UNIT 7

12 CUT OUT. THEN LISTEN AND PLAY.

UNIT 8

12 CUT OUT. THEN LISTEN AND PLAY.

HELLO

UNIT 1 MY BODY

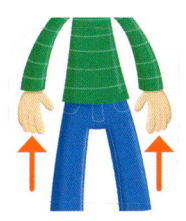

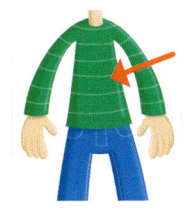

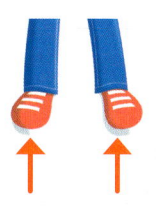

UNIT 2 MY FAMILY

UNIT 3 MY CLASSROOM

UNIT 4 ANIMALS

UNIT 5 THE SEA

UNIT 6 TOYS

UNIT 7 FOOD

UNIT 8 MY VACATION

UNIT 1 MY BODY

UNIT 2 MY FAMILY

UNIT 3 MY CLASSROOM

UNIT 4 ANIMALS

93

| UNIT 5 | THE SEA |

| UNIT 6 | TOYS |

| UNIT 7 | FOOD |

| UNIT 8 | MY VACATION |

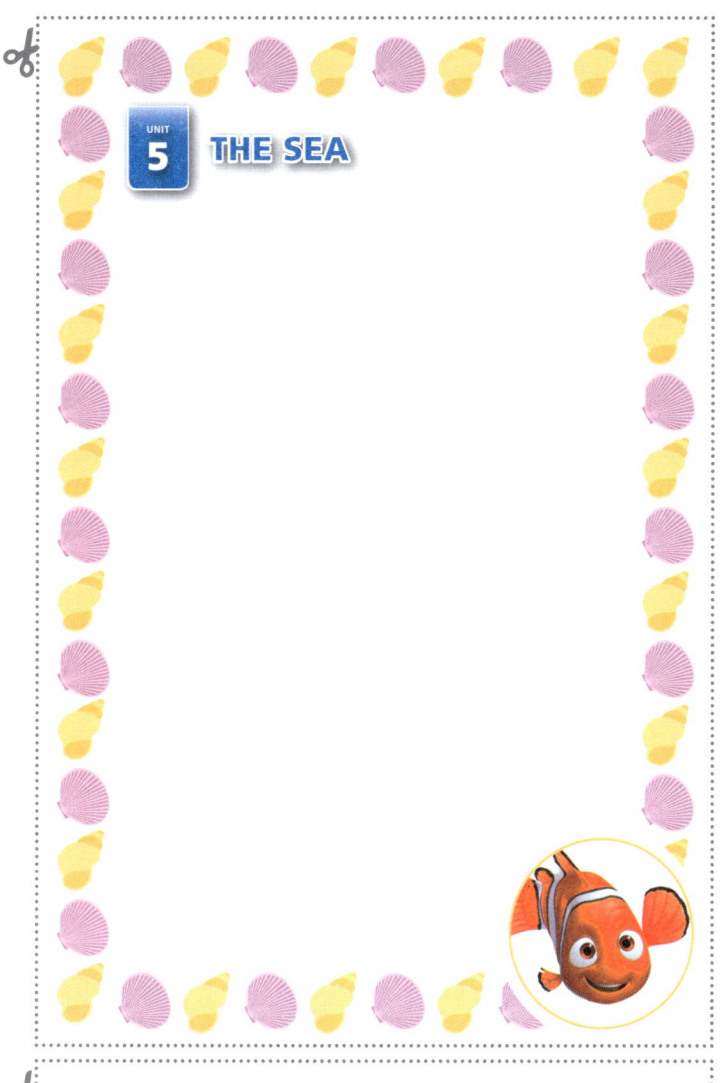

NEW English Adventure

WORKBOOK
LEVEL 1

CONTENTS	PAGE
HELLO	98
1. MY BODY	100
2. MY FAMILY	108
3. MY CLASSROOM	116
4. ANIMALS	124
5. THE SEA	132
6. TOYS	140
7. FOOD	148
8. MY VACATION	156
HAPPY EASTER!	164
MERRY CHRISTMAS!	165
FAMILY DAY	166
PICTURE DICTIONARY	167
STICKERS	169

HELLO

1 COLOR.

2 CHOOSE, FOLLOW AND COLOR.

UNIT 1 MY BODY

1 LOOK AND MATCH.

1   2    3    4

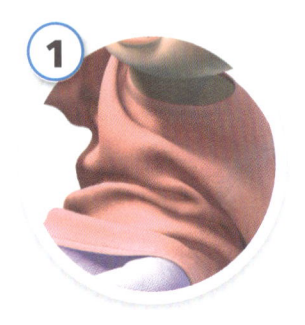

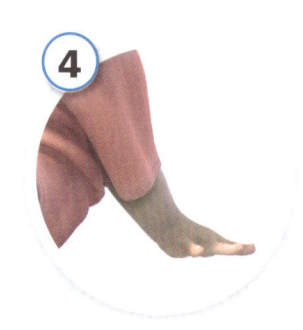

2 FOLLOW AND COLOR.

101

3 COUNT AND MATCH.

1

2

3

4

5

4 FIND AND CIRCLE. THEN COLOR.

5 LOOK AND COLOR.

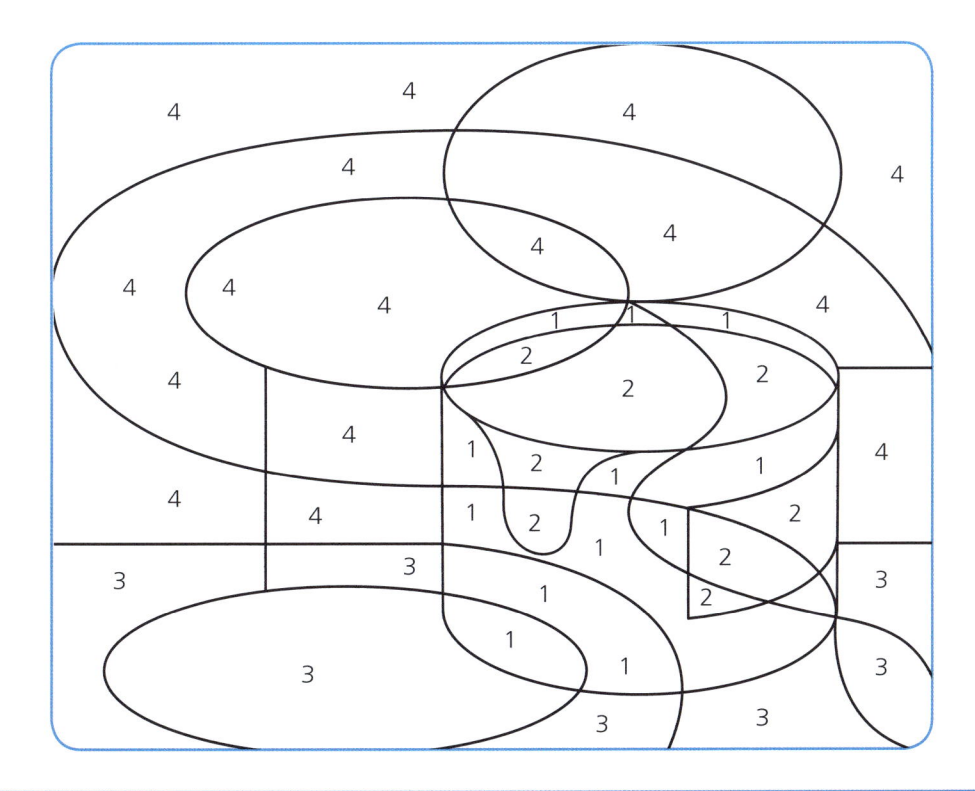

1
2
3
4

6 FIND AND MATCH.

7 FIND, COUNT AND COLOR.

1
2
3
4

8 LOOK AND DRAW.

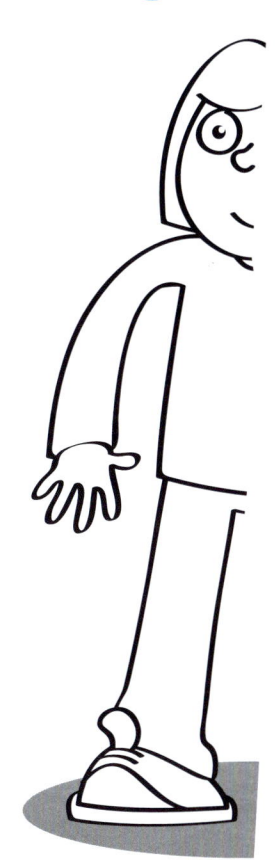

9 DRAW A MONSTER.

UNIT 1
EXTRA ADVENTURE

MY BODY

1 LOOK AND COLOR.

REVIEW 1

1 LOOK AND CHECK (✓) OR CROSS (✗).

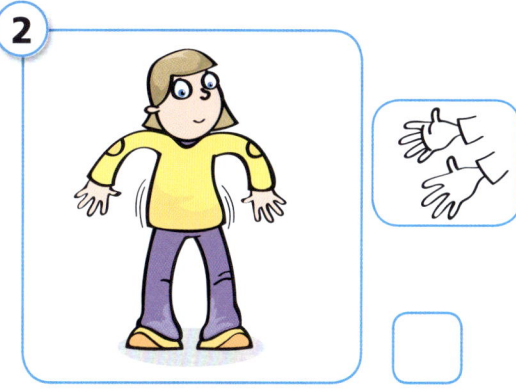

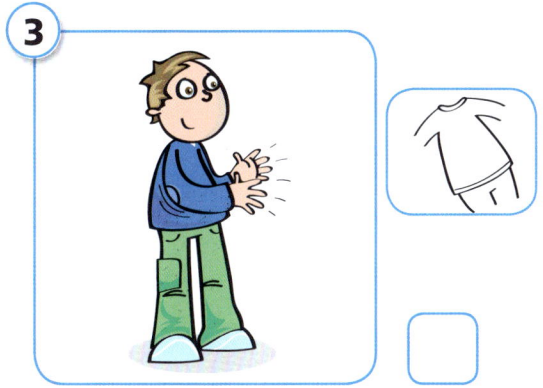

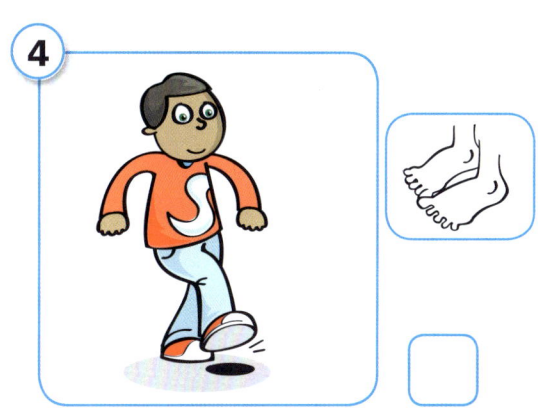

1
2
3
4

2 SAY AND STICK.

107

UNIT 2
MY FAMILY

1 MATCH AND COLOR.

1.
2.
3.
4.
5.
6.

108

2 FOLLOW AND COLOR.

3 FIND AND MATCH.

UNIT 2

4 LOOK AND NUMBER.

1

2

3

5 FIND AND CHECK (✓).

1.

2.

6 LOOK AND MATCH.

1

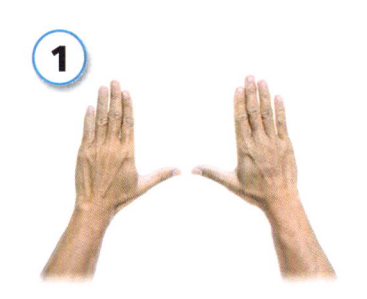

2

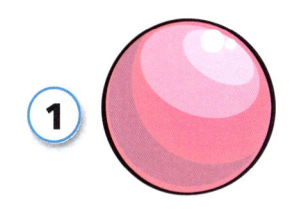

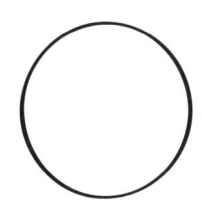

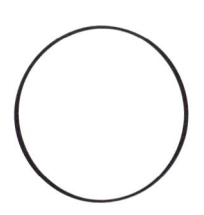

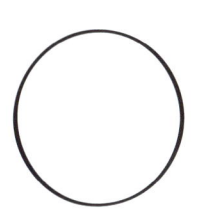

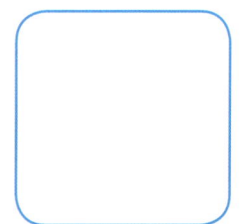

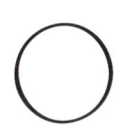

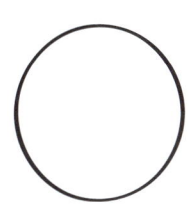

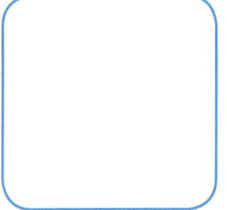

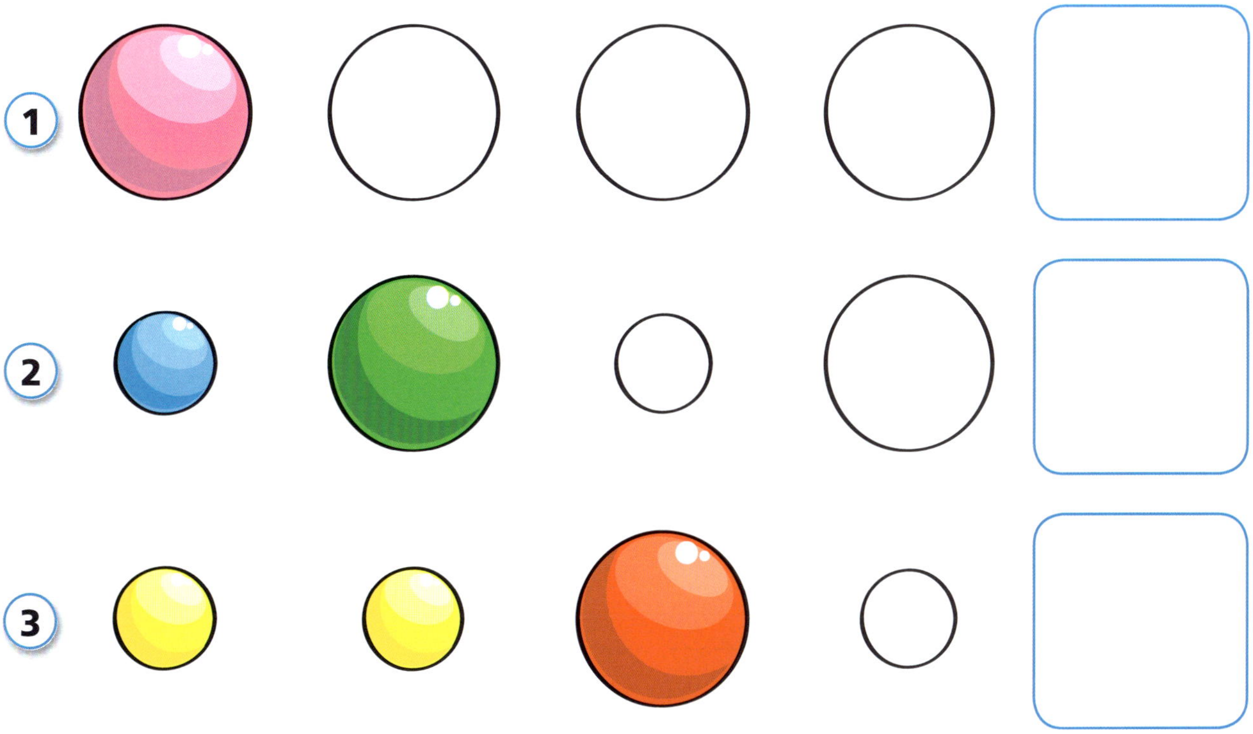

3

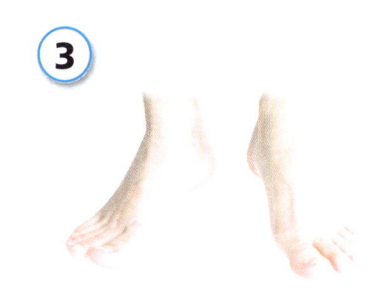

4

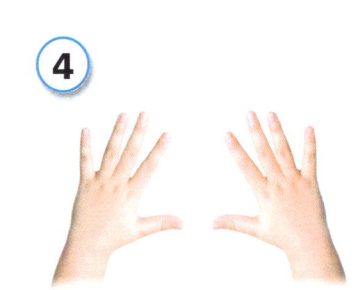

7 FOLLOW THE SEQUENCE AND DRAW. THEN COLOR.

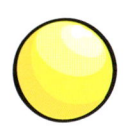

1

2

3

UNIT 2 EXTRA ADVENTURE

MY FAMILY

1 FOLLOW THE SEQUENCE AND DRAW.

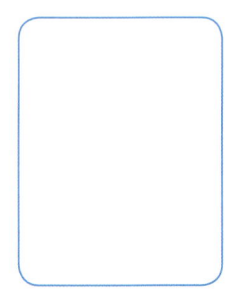

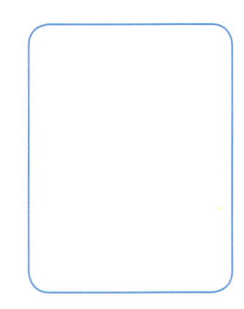

2 TRACE.

Lesson 1: xx

114

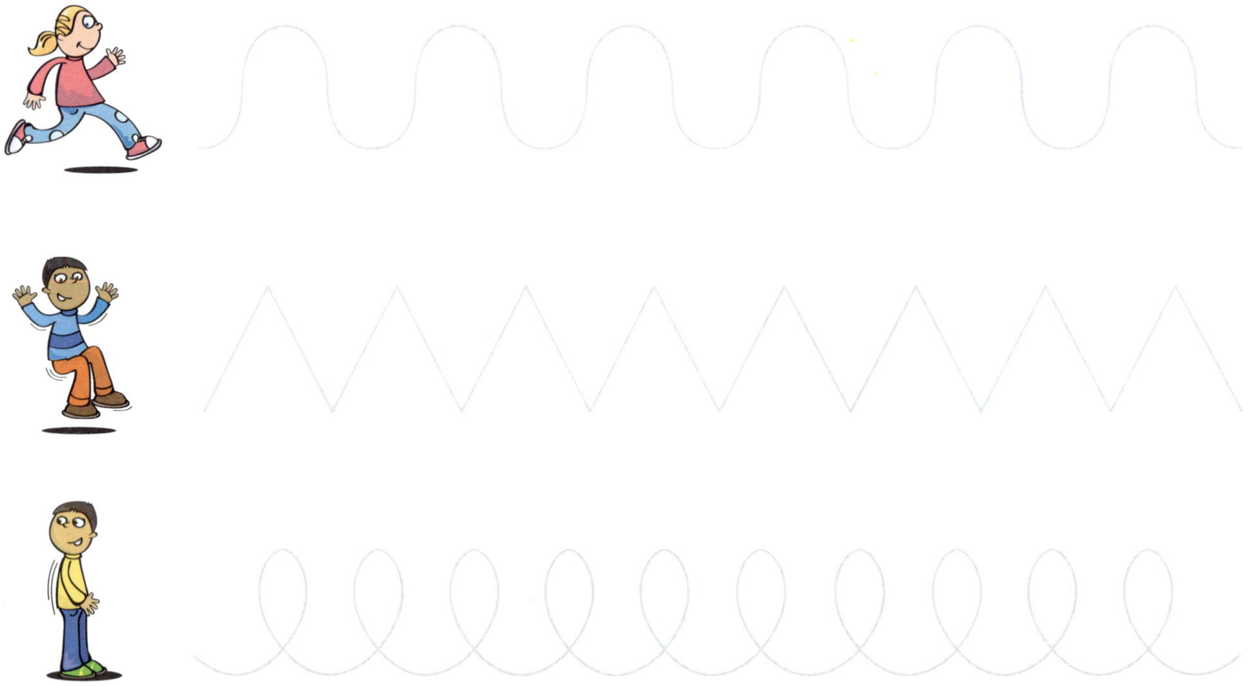

REVIEW 2

1 FIND AND MATCH.

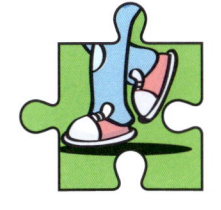

2 SAY AND STICK.

115

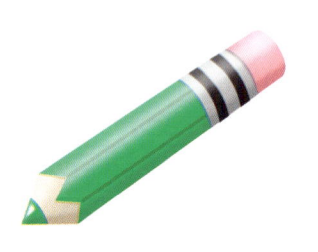

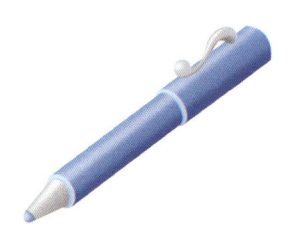

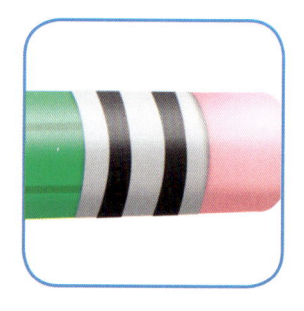

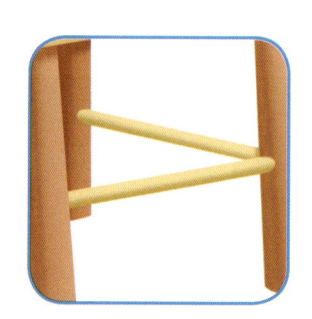

UNIT 3
MY CLASSROOM

1 LOOK AND MATCH.

2 FIND AND COLOR.

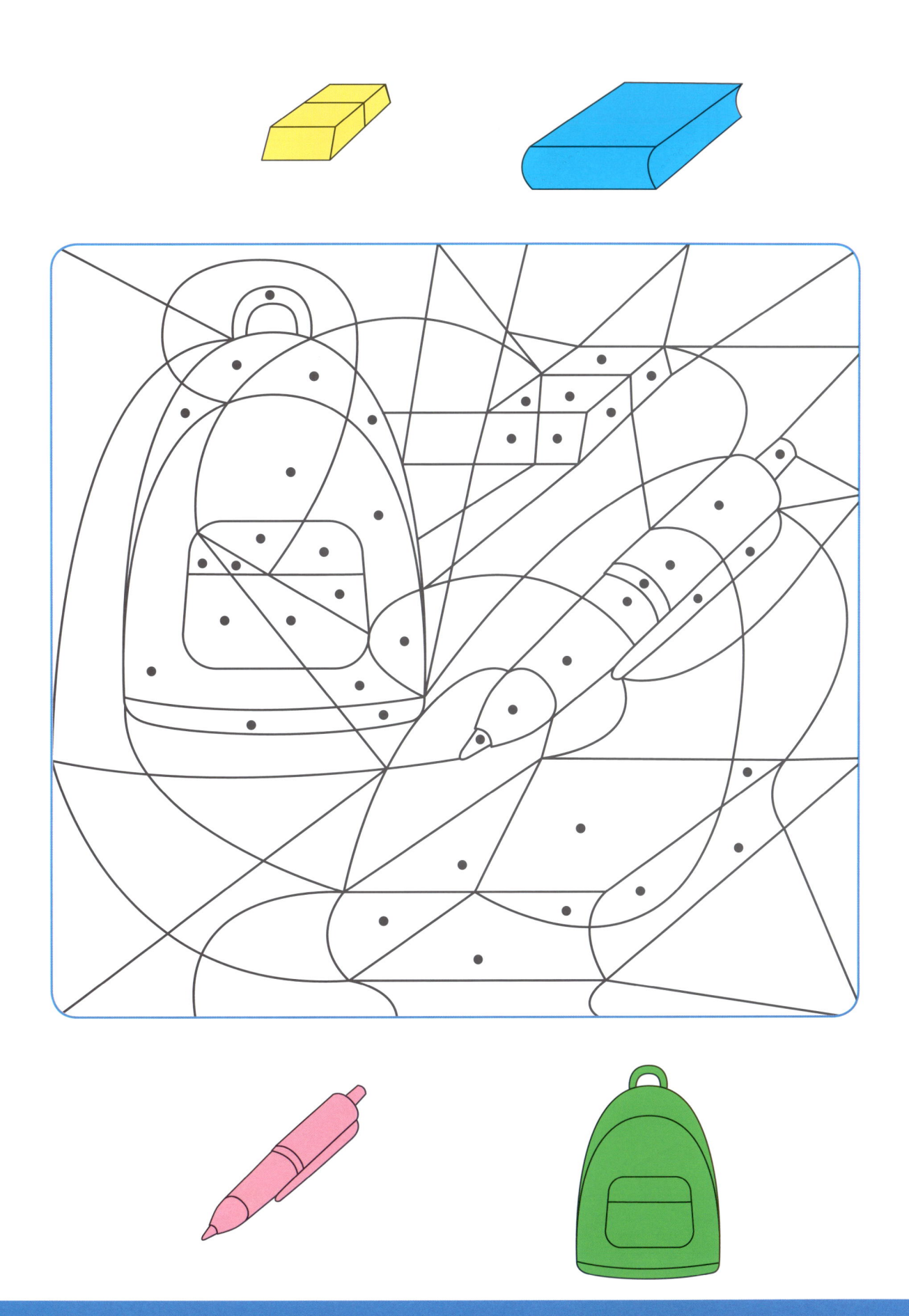

3 LOOK AND DRAW.

4 FIND AND CIRCLE.

1

2

3

5 FOLLOW AND COLOR.

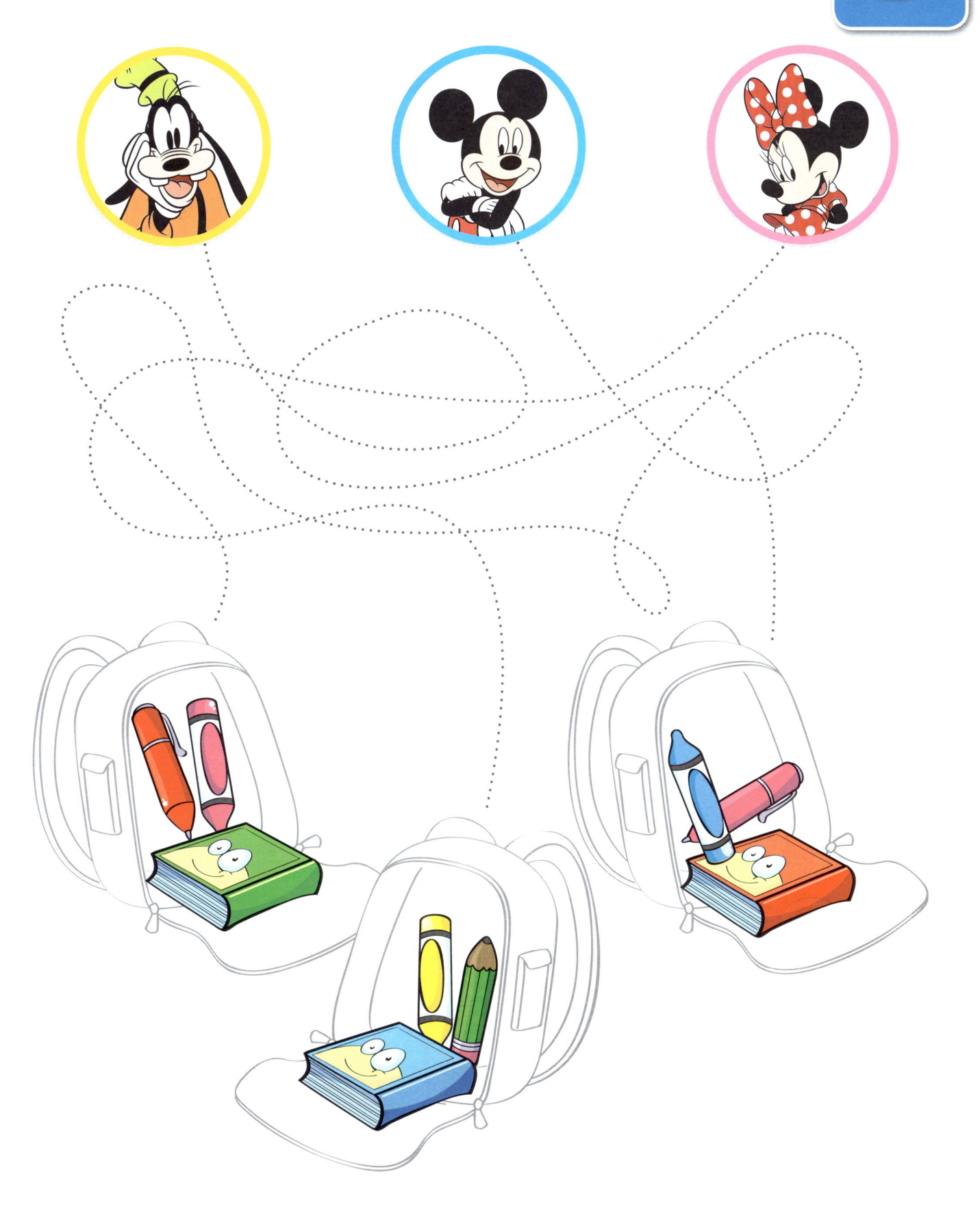

6 FIND THE ODD ONE OUT AND CIRCLE.

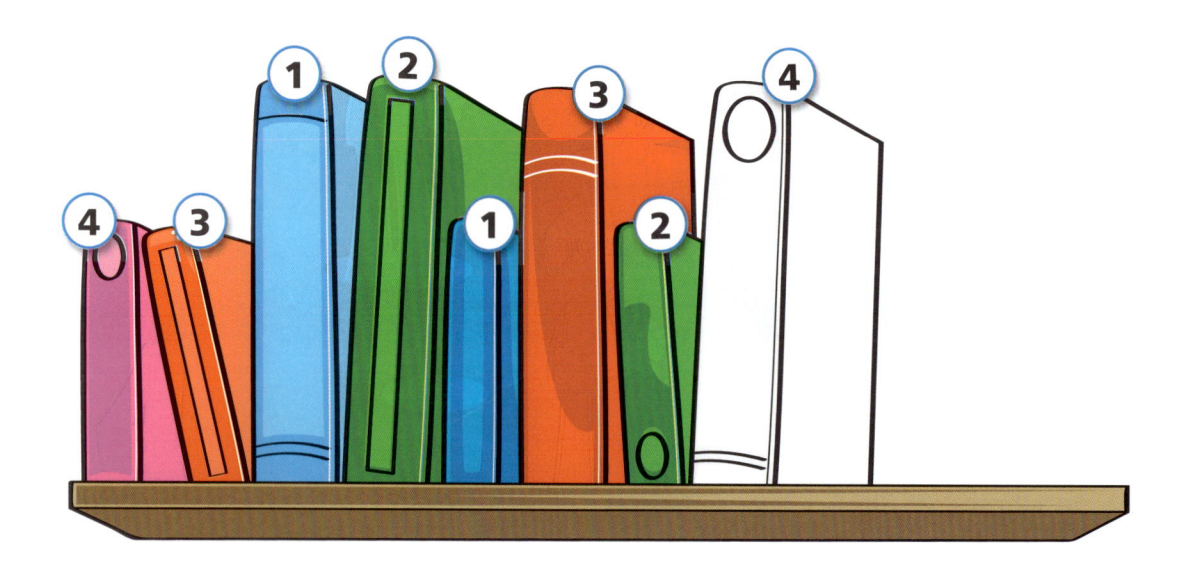

①

②

③

7 FIND AND COLOR.

8 FOLLOW THE SEQUENCE AND COLOR.

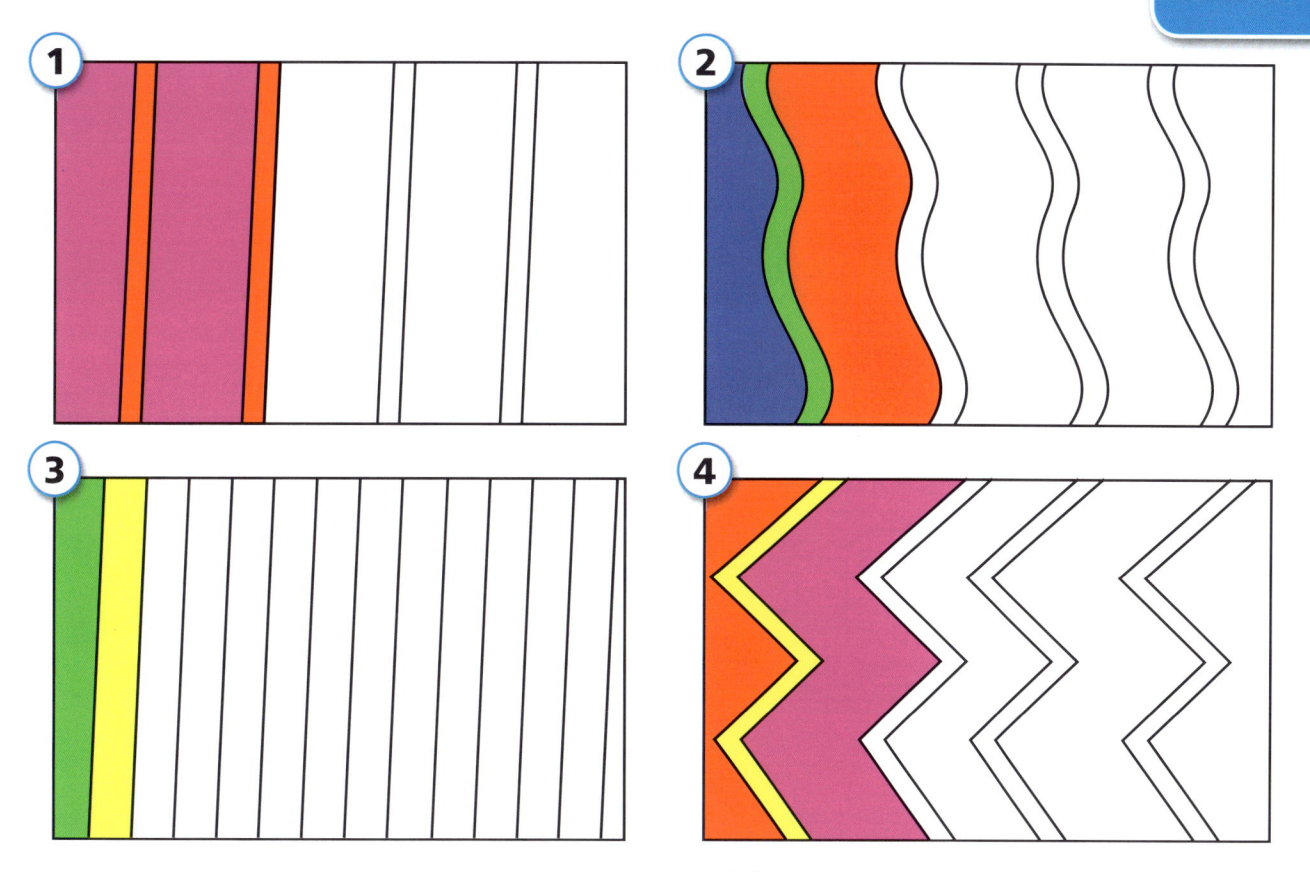

9 LOOK AT THE COLOR AND TRACE.

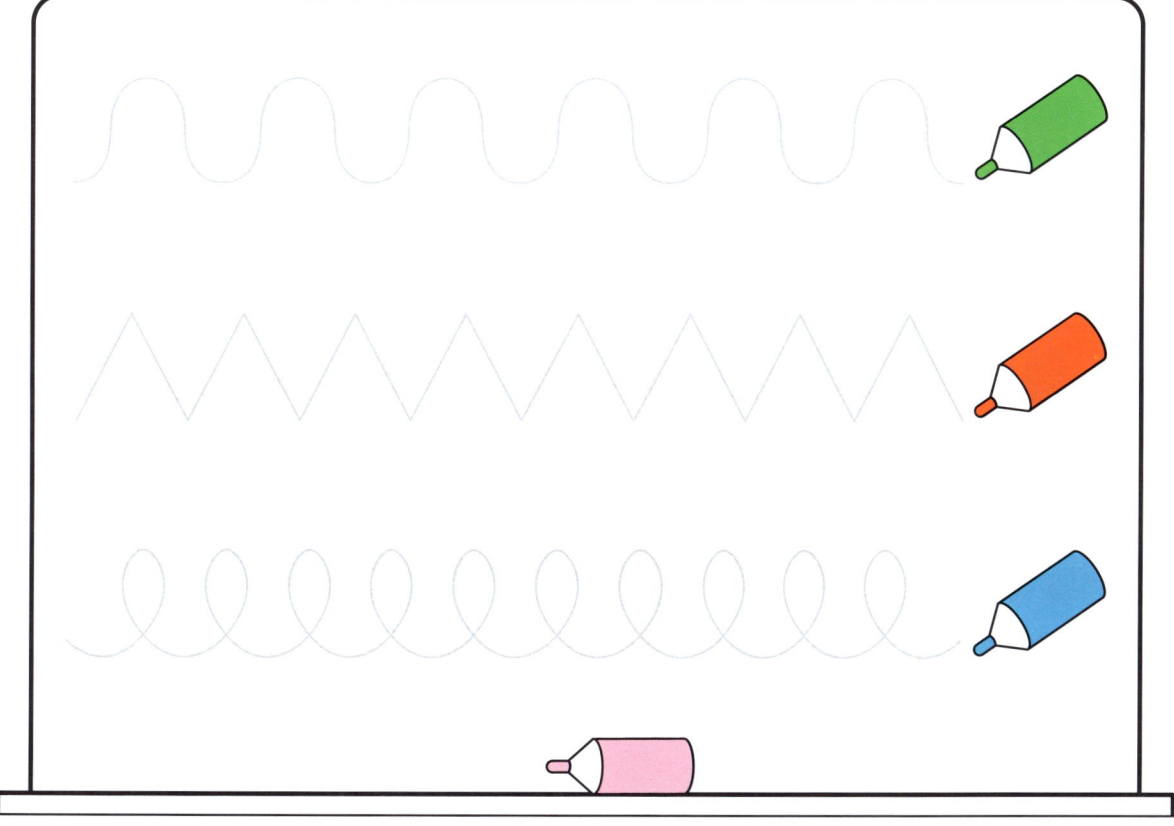

UNIT **3**

121

UNIT 3 — EXTRA ADVENTURE

MY CLASSROOM

1 COUNT AND DRAW ●.

REVIEW 3

1 FIND AND CHECK (✓).

2 SAY AND STICK.

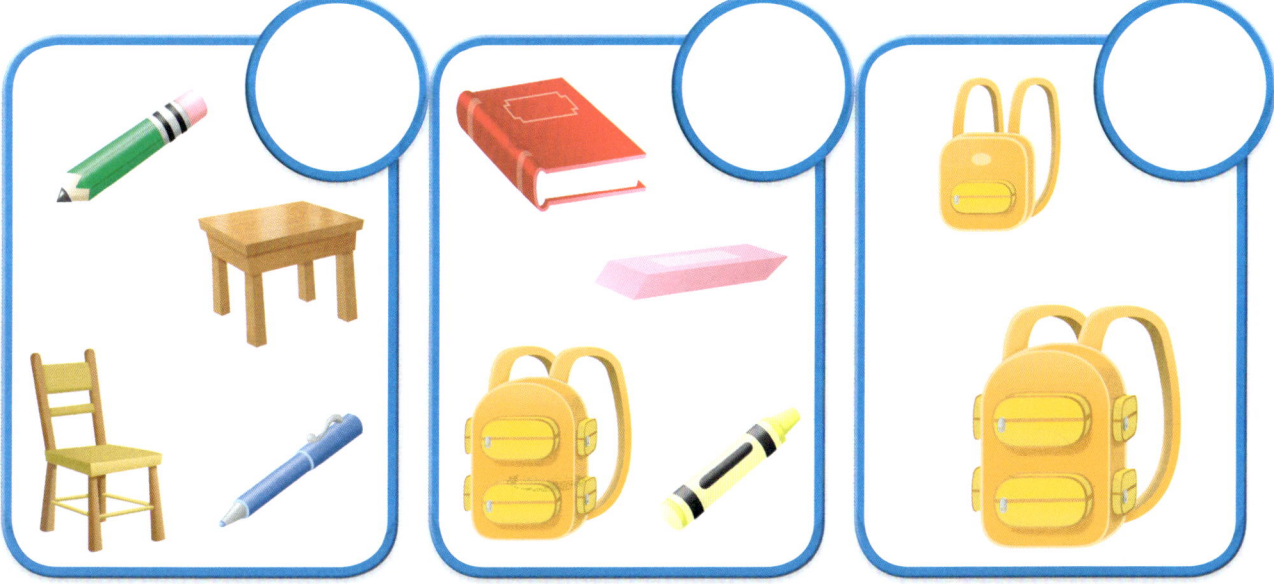

123

UNIT 4 ANIMALS

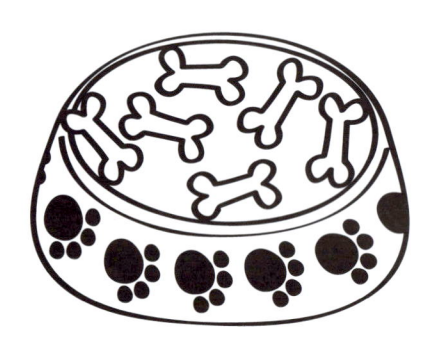

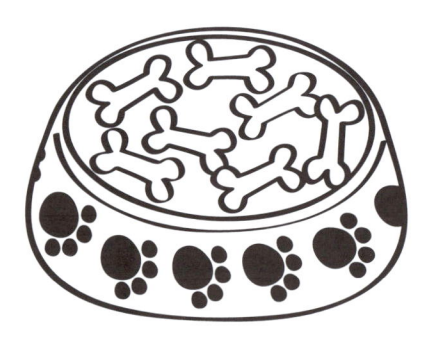

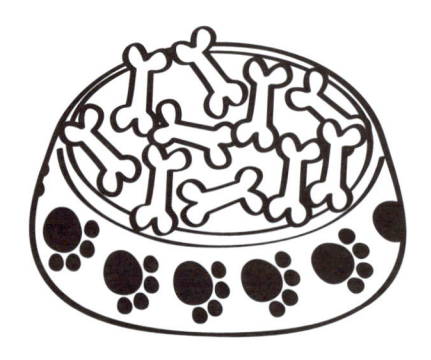

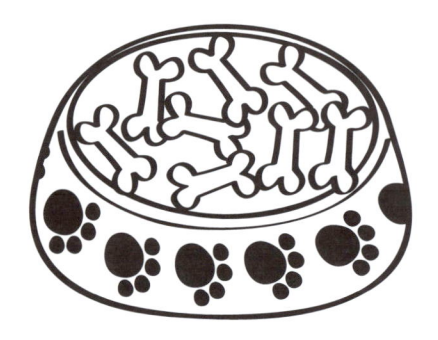

1 FIND, MATCH AND COLOR.

6 8 10

7 9

2 DRAW, MATCH AND COLOR.

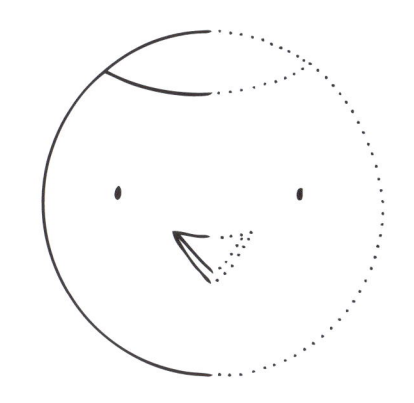

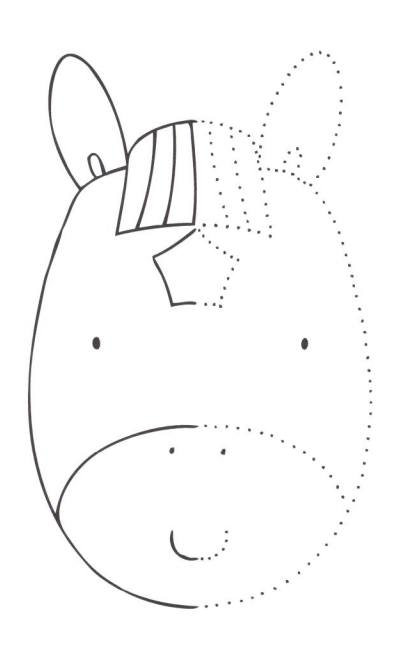

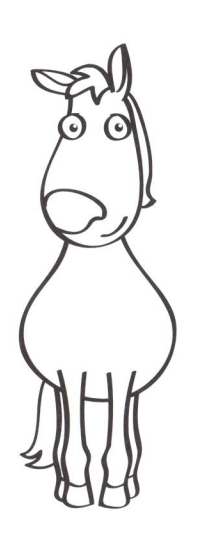

125

3 FOLLOW AND COLOR.

4 LOOK AND DRAW.

126

5 FOLLOW AND COLOR.

UNIT 4

6 COUNT. THEN LOOK AND COLOR.

7 LOOK AND MATCH.

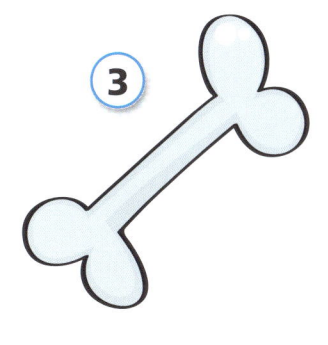

1
2
3
4

8 TRACE AND COLOR.

129

UNIT 4 EXTRA ADVENTURE

ANIMALS

1 FIND AND COUNT. THEN COLOR.

1

2

3

REVIEW 4

1 FOLLOW, MATCH AND COLOR.

1.
2.
3.
4.

2 SAY AND STICK.

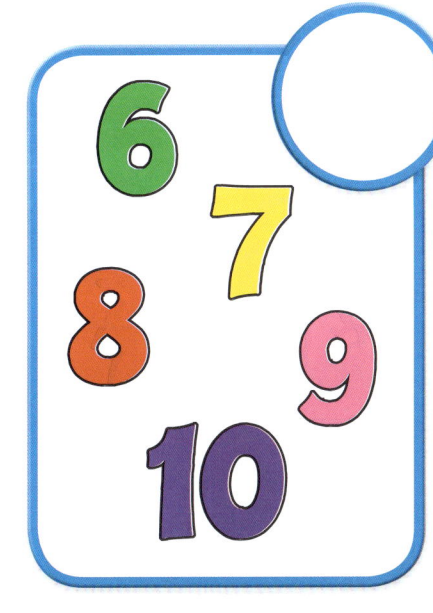

131

UNIT 5 THE SEA

1 JOIN THE DOTS. THEN CIRCLE.

2 FIND AND COLOR.

3 LOOK AND COLOR.

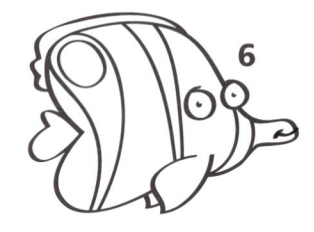

1. orange
2. purple
3. pink
4. brown
5. green
6. blue

4 COUNT AND COLOR.

5 FOLLOW AND COLOR.

6 CIRCLE THE ODD ONE OUT.

1

2

3

135

7 FIND AND CIRCLE 6 DIFFERENCES.

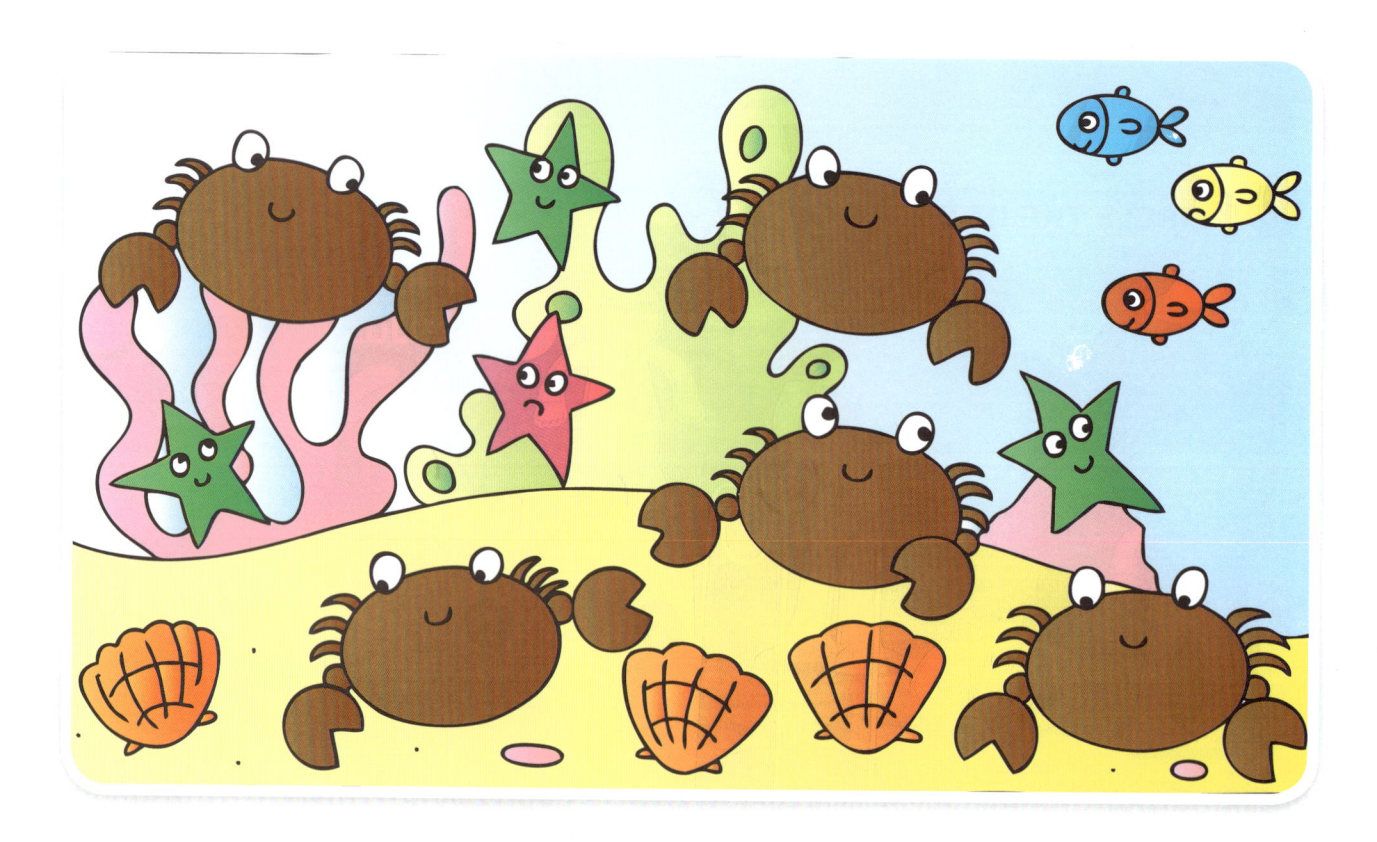

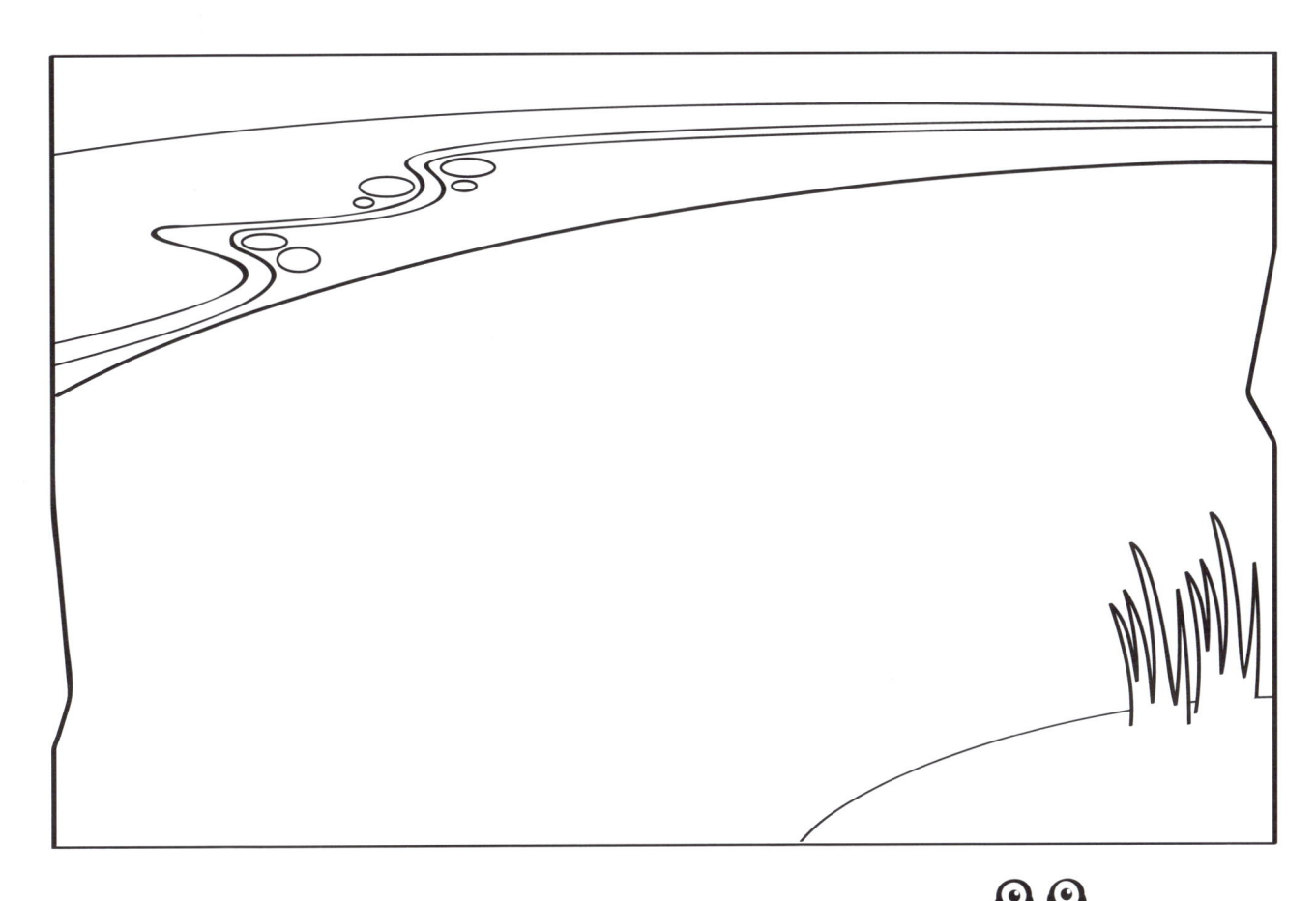

8 CIRCLE OR CROSS OUT. THEN DRAW AND COLOR.

UNIT 5
EXTRA ADVENTURE

THE SEA

1 FIND AND COLOR.

2 COUNT AND CIRCLE.

4 / 5

3 / 6

8 / 6

1 / 2

Lesson 1: xx

138

REVIEW 5

1 LOOK AND COLOR.

1 2 3 4 5 6 7

2 SAY AND STICK.

Lesson 2: 3

139

UNIT 6 — TOYS

1 FIND AND CIRCLE. THEN DRAW AND COLOR.

140

2 FIND AND MATCH. THEN COLOR.

141

3 TRACE AND COLOR.

4 FIND AND CIRCLE 4 DIFFERENCES.

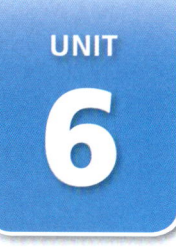

5 FIND AND MATCH. THEN COLOR.

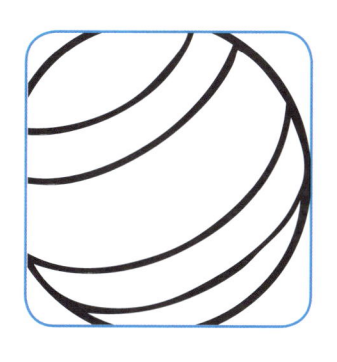

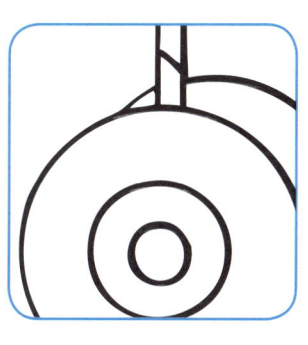

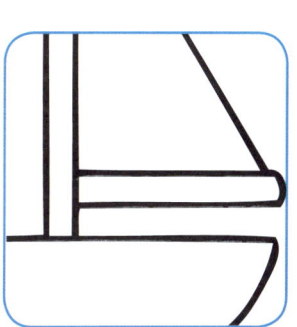

143

6 COUNT, CIRCLE AND COLOR.

3 4   1 2   6 3

UNIT 6

7 FOLLOW AND COLOR.

1
2
3

8 MATCH AND DRAW.

145

UNIT 6 EXTRA ADVENTURE

TOYS

1 LOOK AND DRAW. THEN COLOR.

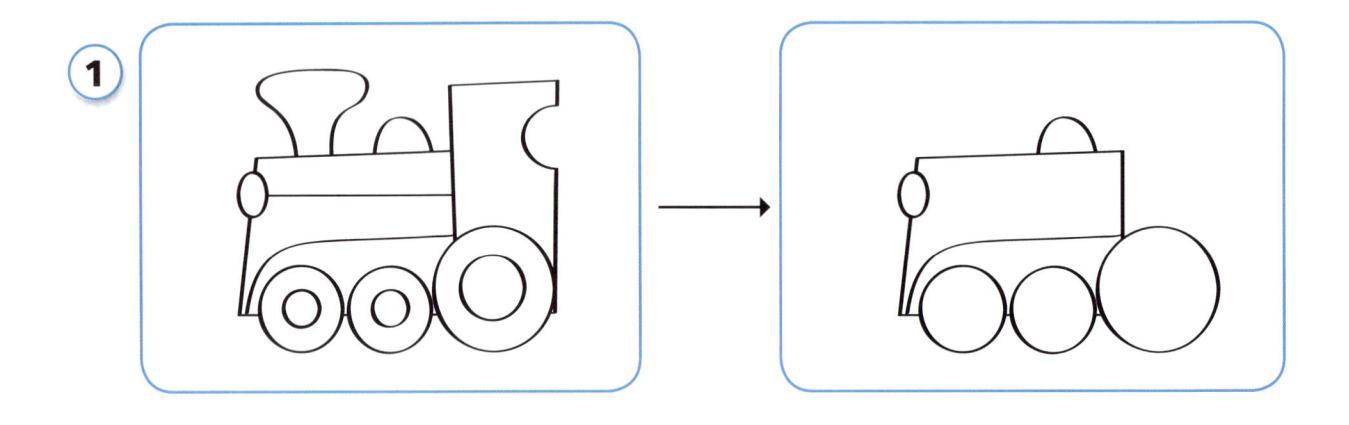

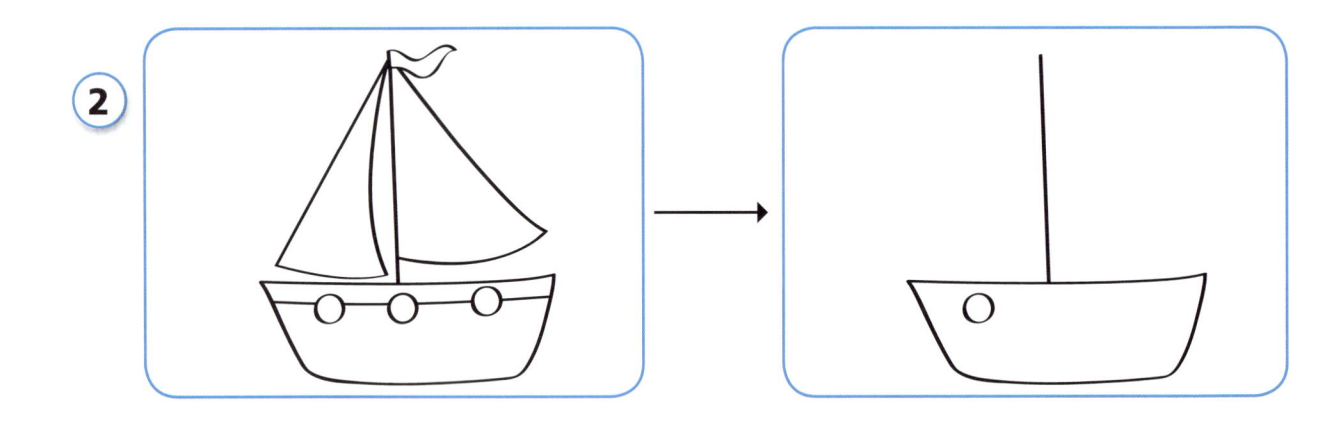

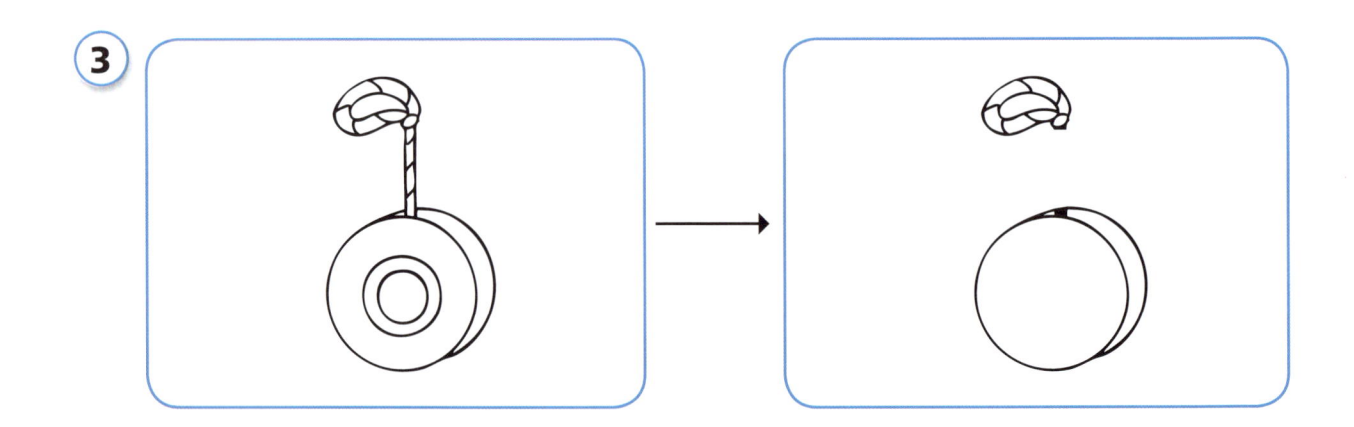

1.

2.

3.

146

REVIEW 6

1 FIND AND DRAW.

2 SAY AND STICK.

147

UNIT 7 FOOD

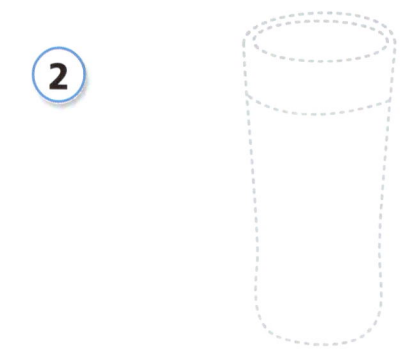

1 TRACE AND COLOR.

1.
2.
3.
4.

2 FOLLOW AND COLOR.

148

3 COUNT AND MATCH.

2

3

4

5

4 COUNT AND DRAW.

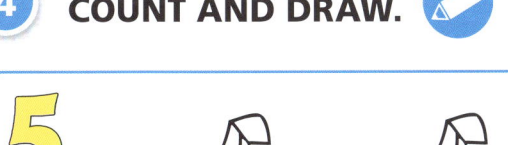

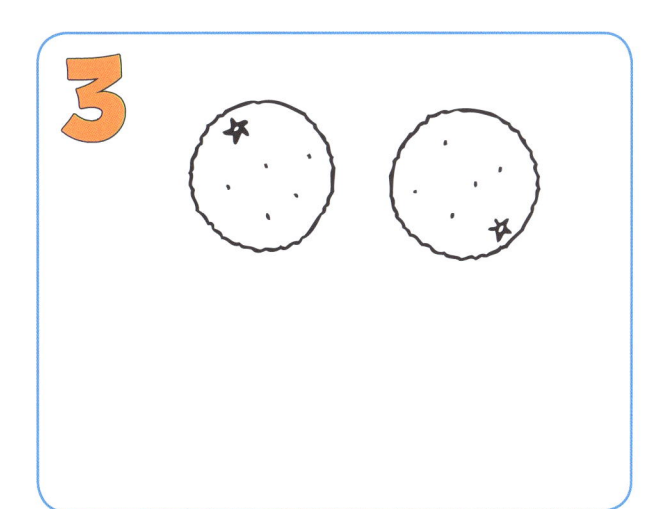

5

3

4

6

5 FIND AND CHECK (✓) OR CROSS (✗).

6 FIND AND CIRCLE.

7 FIND THE ODD ONE OUT AND CROSS OUT.

151

8 FIND AND COLOR.

9 READ AND CIRCLE.

1. I LIKE PEARS. / I DON'T LIKE PEARS.

2. I LIKE CAKES. / I DON'T LIKE CAKES.

10 LOOK AND DRAW.

1

2

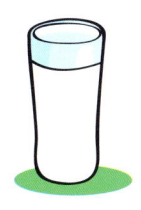

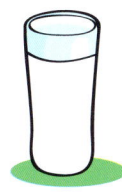

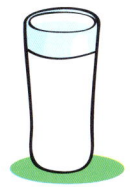

3

11 FIND THE ODD ONE OUT AND CROSS OUT. THEN COLOR.

153

UNIT 7

EXTRA ADVENTURE

FOOD

1 FOLLOW. THEN DRAW AND COLOR.

REVIEW 7

1 MATCH AND COLOR. THEN DRAW 😊 OR ☹.

2 SAY AND STICK.

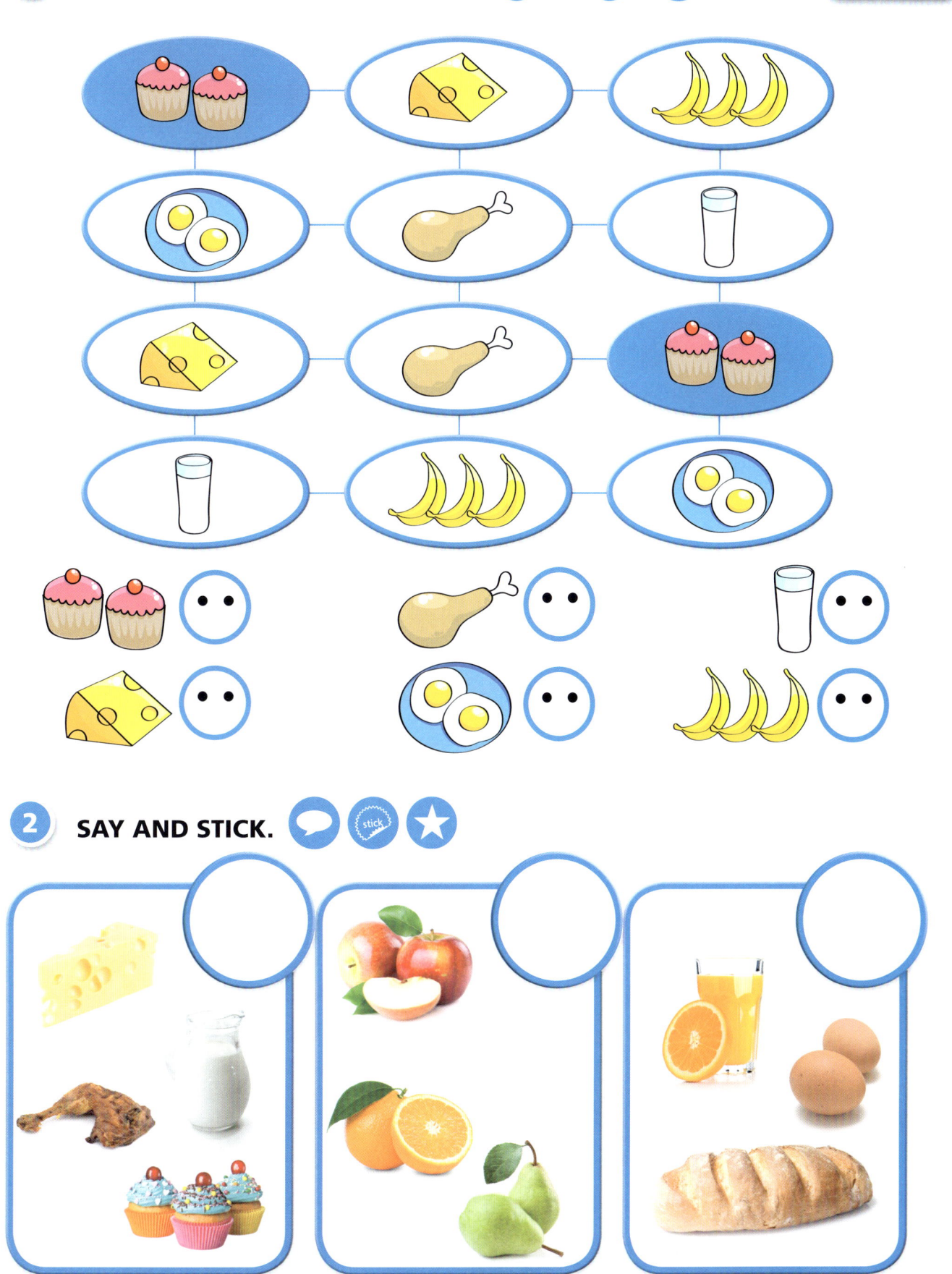

UNIT 8
MY VACATION

1 LOOK AND CHECK (✓). THEN COLOR.

2 LOOK AND DRAW.

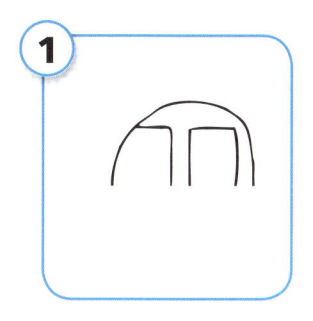

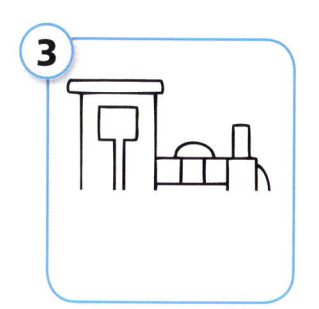

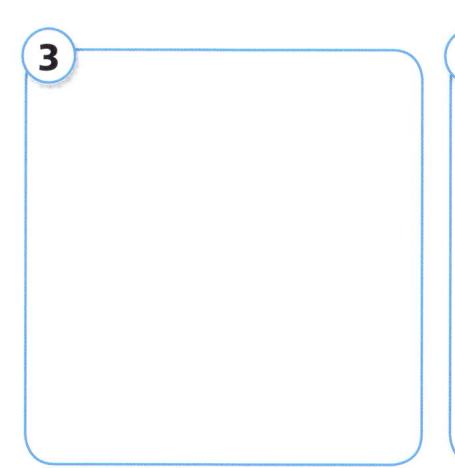

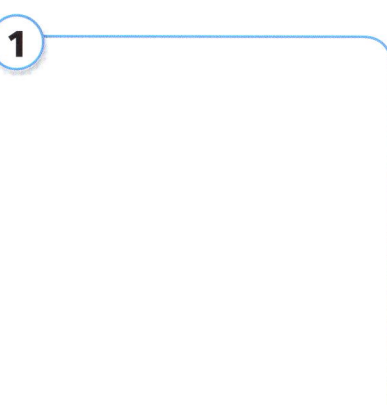

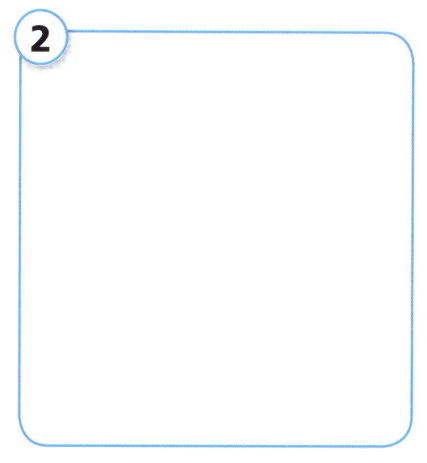

1

2

3

3

1

2

3 FIND AND COLOR.

4 FIND AND CIRCLE 7 DIFFERENCES.

5 CHOOSE AND DRAW. THEN COLOR.

UNIT 8

6. LOOK AND DRAW.

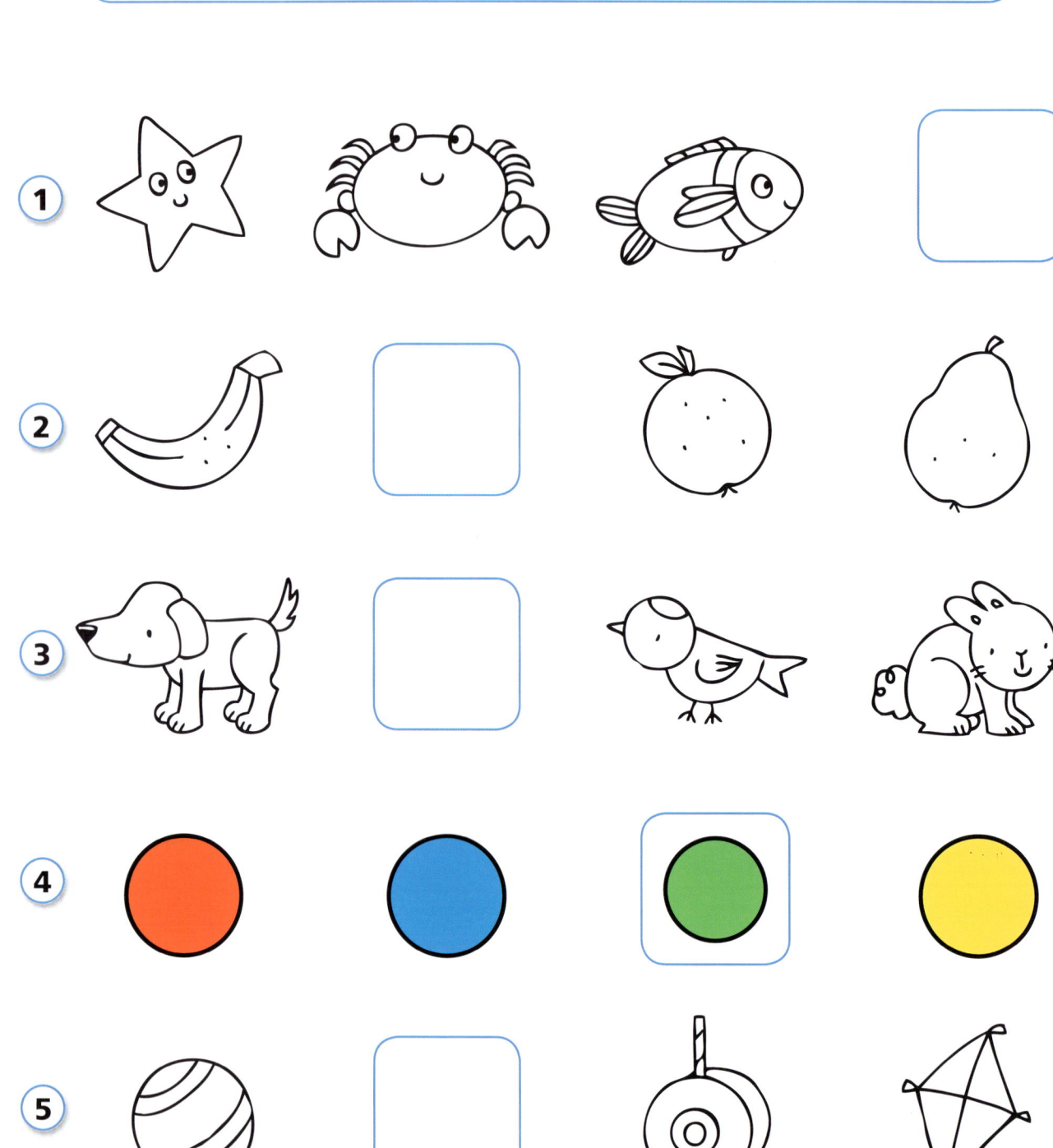

1.
2.
3.
4.
5.

7 LOOK AND MATCH.

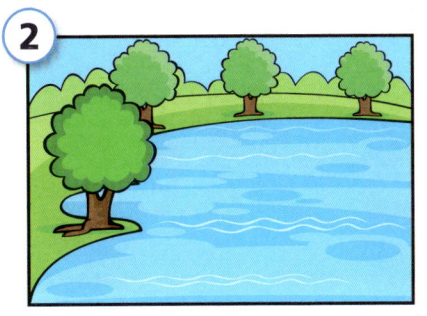

1
2
3

8 COLOR.

UNIT 8 EXTRA ADVENTURE

MY VACATION

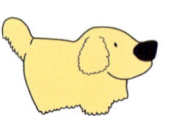

1 FIND AND DRAW.

REVIEW 8

1 COUNT, MATCH AND CIRCLE.

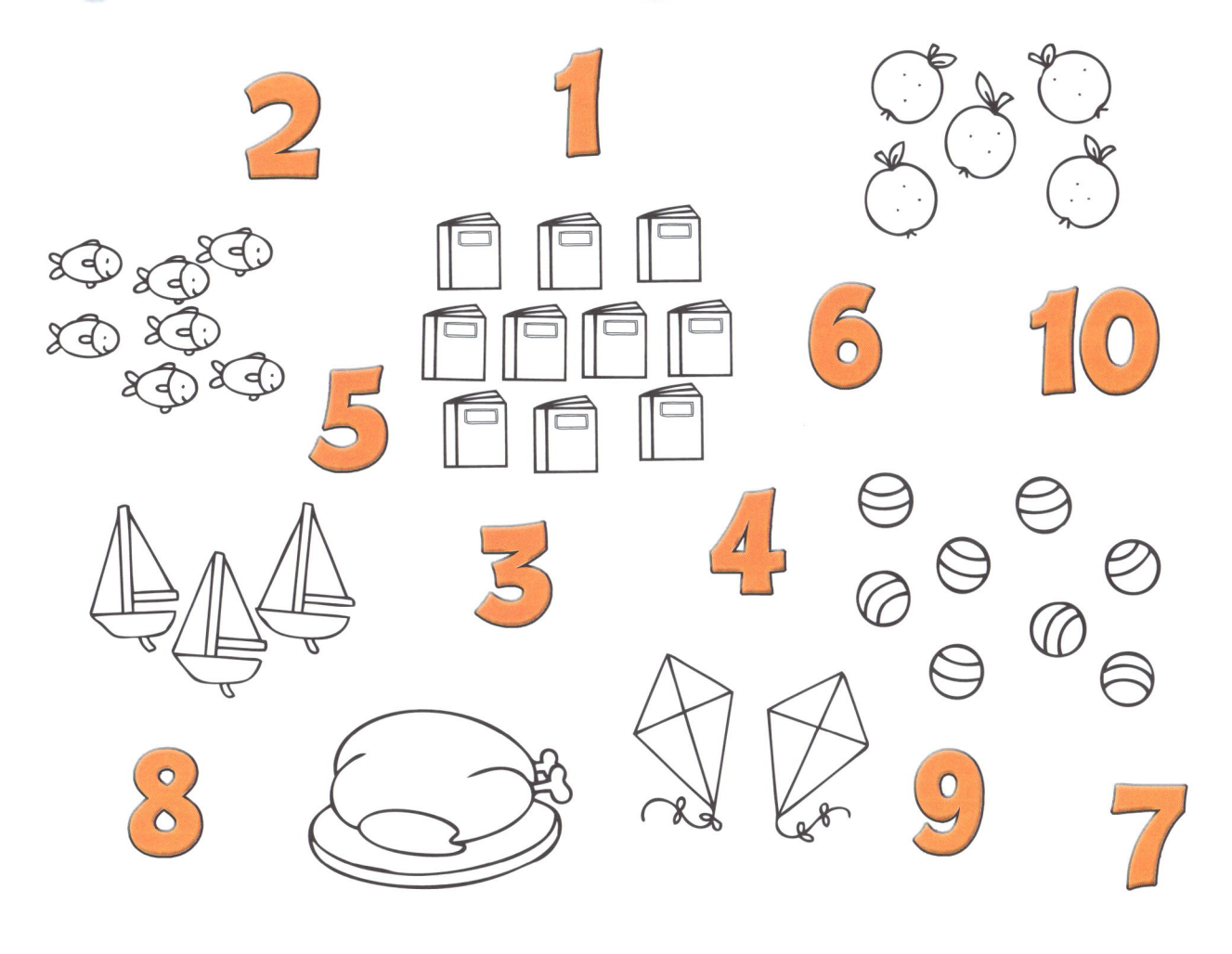

2   1
5   6   10
3   4
8   9   7

2 SAY AND STICK.

HAPPY EASTER!

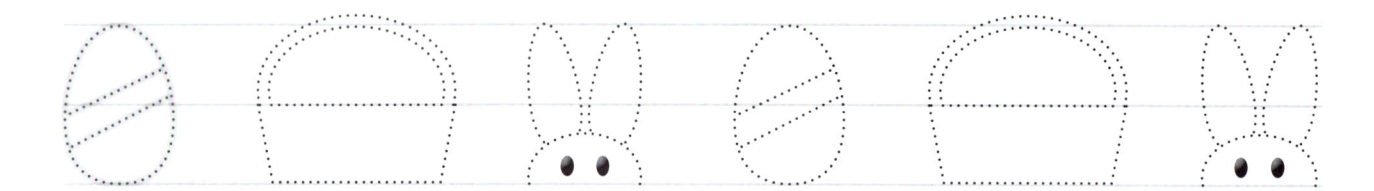

1 TRACE AND COLOR.

2 COUNT AND MATCH. THEN COLOR.

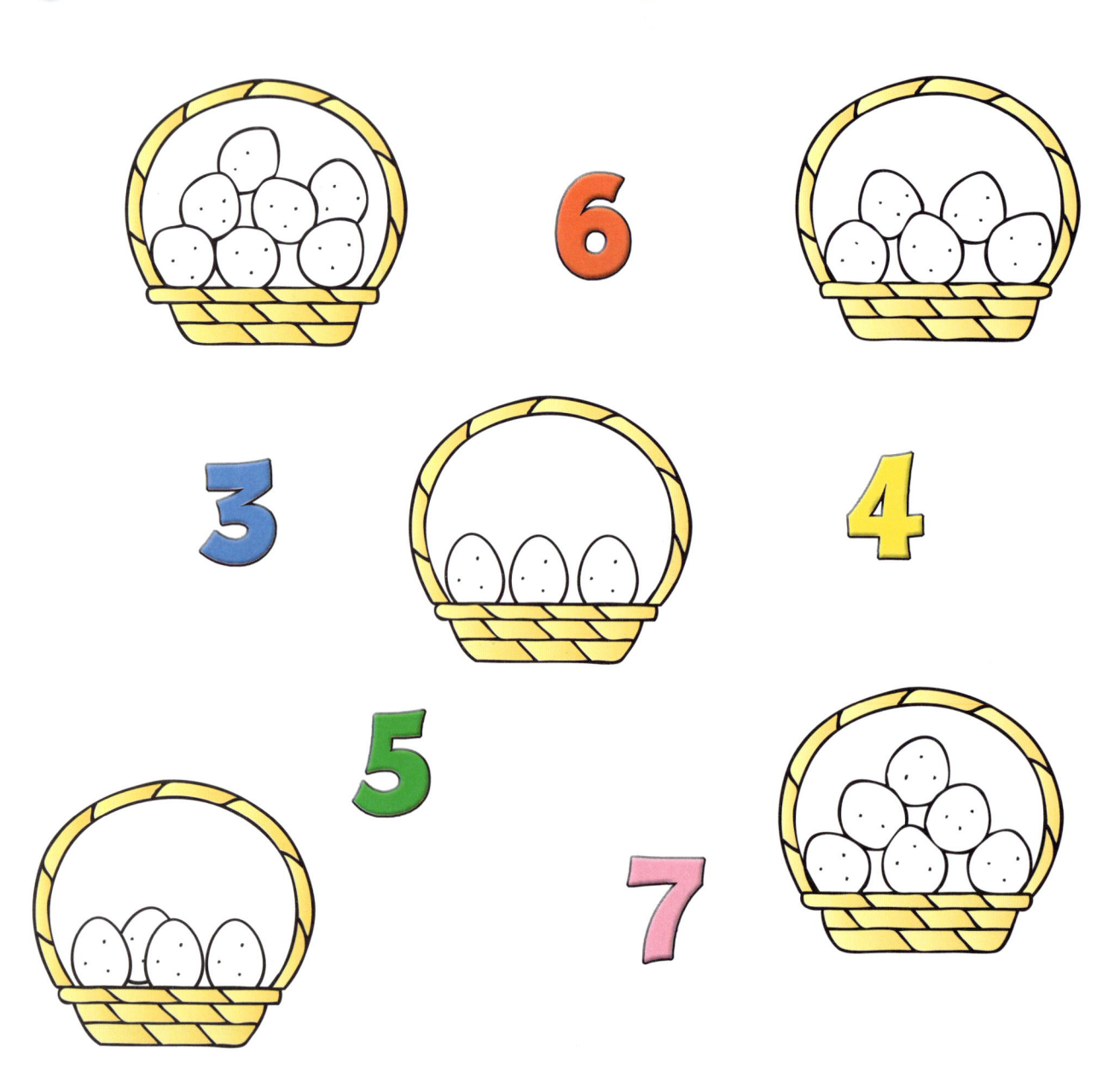

MERRY CHRISTMAS!

1 FIND THE ODD ONE OUT AND CIRCLE.

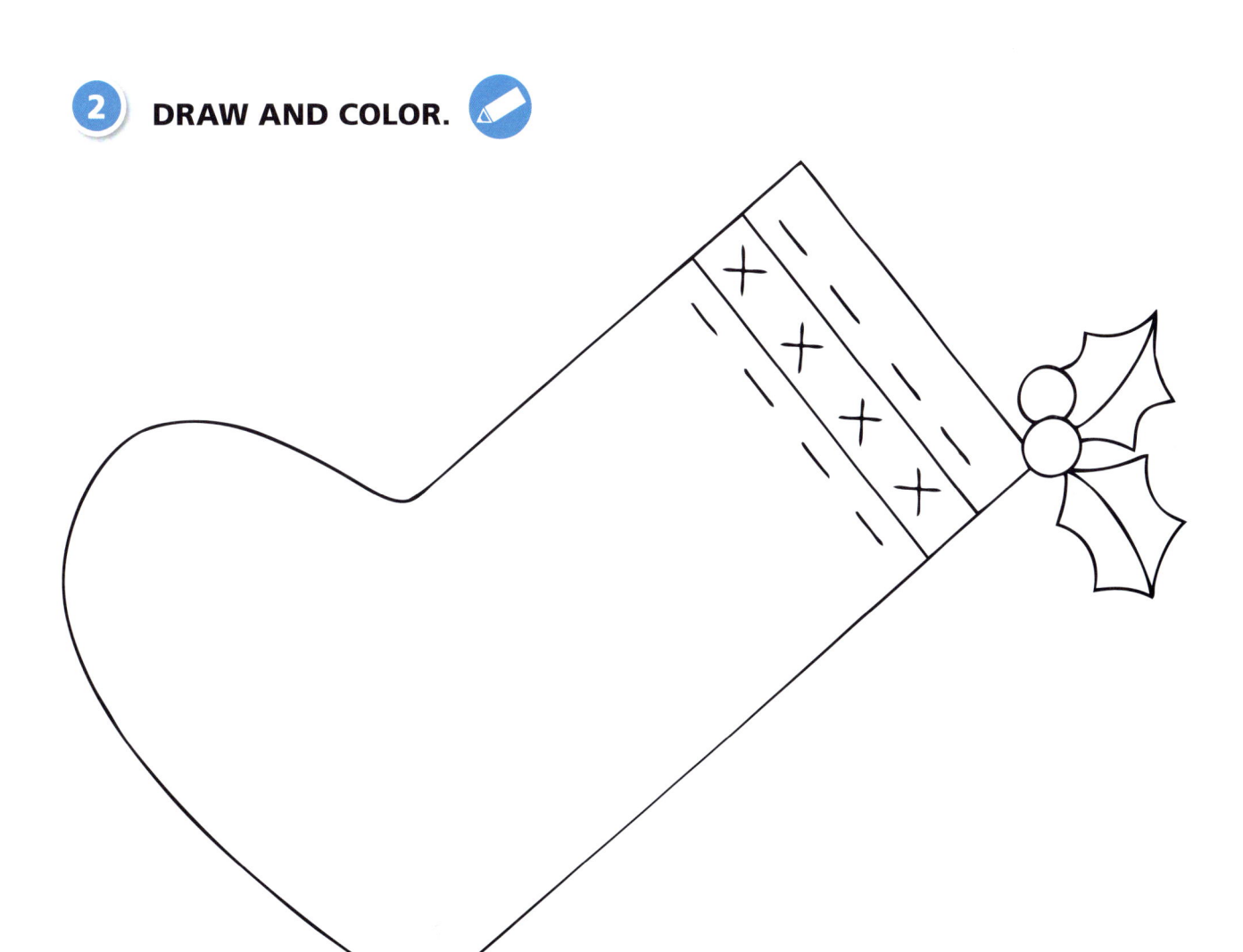

2 DRAW AND COLOR.

FAMILY DAY

1 FIND AND COLOR.

2 LOOK AND MATCH.

PICTURE DICTIONARY

HELLO

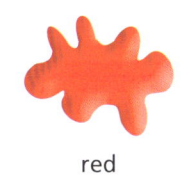

blue green pink red yellow

UNIT 1 MY BODY

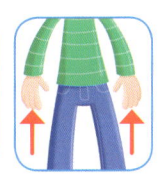

body feet hands head one two three four five

UNIT 2 MY FAMILY

BROTHER DAD FRIEND GRANDMA GRANDPA MOM SISTER

UNIT 3 MY CLASSROOM

BAG BOOK CHAIR CRAYON PEN PENCIL ERASER TABLE

UNIT 4 ANIMALS

BIRD CAT DOG HORSE RABBIT

SIX SEVEN EIGHT NINE TEN

BLACK WHITE

UNIT 5 THE SEA

CRAB FISH OCTOPUS SEAHORSE SHELL STARFISH TURTLE

BROWN GRAY ORANGE PURPLE HAPPY SAD

UNIT 6 TOYS

BALL BOAT CAR DOLL KITE TEDDY BEAR TRAIN YO-YO

UNIT 7 FOOD

APPLES BANANAS BREAD CAKES CHEESE CHICKEN EGGS JUICE MILK ORANGES PEARS

UNIT 8 MY VACATION

BEACH  SANDCASTLE  SEA

MERRY CHRISTMAS!

BELL CHRISTMAS CARD CHRISTMAS TREE SANTA CLAUS PRESENT STOCKING

HAPPY EASTER!

CHICK EASTER EGG BASKET EASTER BUNNY

FAMILY DAY

CARD FLOWER PRESENT

UNIT 1 MY BODY

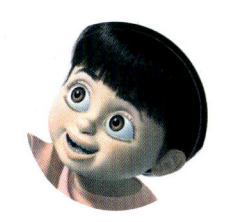

UNIT 2 MY FAMILY

UNIT 3 MY CLASSROOM

UNIT 4 ANIMALS

UNIT 5 THE SEA

UNIT 6 TOYS     **UNIT 7 FOOD**     **UNIT 8 MY VACATION**